CP/M® for the IBM:
Using CP/M-86®

Chapters 10 thru 14

**MORE THAN TWO MILLION PEOPLE HAVE LEARNED
TO PROGRAM, USE, AND ENJOY MICROCOMPUTERS WITH
WILEY PRESS GUIDES.**

The Wiley IBM PC Series
Laurence Press, Series Editor

*Communications on the IBM PC,** Schwaderer
 CP/M® for the IBM: Using CP/M-86®, Fernandez & Ashley
*IBM PC Applications Book,** Press
 IBM PC: Data File Programming, Brown & Finkel
*Management Science on the IBM PC,** Hesse
 PC DOS: Using the IBM PC Operating System, Ashley & Fernandez
 PC Graphics: Charts, Graphs, Games, & Art on the IBM PC, Conklin
*What If . . . : A Guide to Using Electronic Work Sheets on the IBM PC,**
     Williams
*Word Processing on the IBM PC,** Hewes

CP/M® for the IBM: Using CP/M-86®

Judi N. Fernandez
Ruth Ashley
Co-Presidents
DuoTech

Wiley IBM PC Series: Series Editor, Laurence Press, Ph.D.

A Wiley Press Book
JOHN WILEY & SONS, INC.
New York · Chichester · Brisbane · Toronto · Singapore

Publisher: Judy V. Wilson
Editor: Dianne Littwin
Managing Editor: Maria Colligan
Composition and Make-up: Cobb/Dunlop, Inc.

Library of Congress Cataloging in Publication Data

Fernandez, Judi N., 1941-
    CP/M® for the IBM: Using CP/M-86®

    (A Self-teaching guide) (Wiley IBM PC series)
    Includes index.
    1. IBM Personal Computer—Programming. 2. CPM-86
(Computer operating system) I. Ashley, Ruth.
II. Title. III. Title: CP/M® for the IBM:
Using CP/M-86®. IV. Series. V. Series: Wiley IBM
PC series.
QA76.8.I2594F47 1983 001.64'25 82-25619
ISBN 0-471-89719-1 (pbk.)

Printed in the United States of America

83 84 85 10 9 8 7 6 5 4 3 2 1

To the Reader

About CP/M-86

CP/M-86—Control Program/Microcomputers-86—is a disk operating system for microcomputers based on the 8086 microprocessor chip. It is a software package developed by Digital Research of Pacific Grove, California. Its 8-bit counterpart, CP/M, has become the most common microcomputer operating system. Many commercially available software packages run under CP/M-86.

An operating system is a set of programs that help you operate the computer and perform routine work functions. The CP/M-86 system includes programs that allow you to run other programs, create files, erase files, copy files, translate and test 8086 Assembly Language programs, print data from files, display the directory of a disk, and so on. Without CP/M-86 or a similar operating system, it would be very difficult and tedious for you to perform even the most trivial task on your computer.

This book assumes that you have an IBM Personal Computer and a CP/M-86 package. Our intent is not to help you select a system, but to help you use what you already have. If you do not yet have your system, but have selected the machine and CP/M-86, you will still benefit from studying this book. You will need to skip the machine exercises and come back to them when your system has been installed.

This book presents the basic CP/M-86 package. Other manufacturers may have adapted CP/M-86 to serve additional needs. They will, however, most likely have added functions. Most of what is presented in this book should work on any IBM CP/M-86 system. For extra features, study the manuals that arrived with your system—after you have finished this book.

There will be more versions of CP/M-86 released in the future. Each new release is an upgrade of earlier releases. Nothing is lost, but some features may be changed as well as new features added.

How to Use This Book

This Self-Teaching Guide consists of 11 chapters that have been carefully sequenced to introduce you to the IBM Personal Computer and CP/M-86 and help you develop a useful set of skills. We have made every effort to organize the material in the best possible learning sequence, so that you can begin using CP/M-86 as quickly as possible. We strongly recommend that you study the chapters in order. You will learn to do easy tasks, then successively more complex tasks, until you have mastered the system.

Each chapter begins with a short introduction followed by objectives, which outline what you can expect to learn from it, and ends with a Self-Test, which allows you to measure your learning and practice what you have studied. Each chapter also contains a Suggested Machine Exercise that guides you in transferring your new knowledge to the real, hands-on environment.

The body of each chapter is divided into frames—short numbered sections in which information is presented or reviewed, followed by questions which ask you to apply the information. The correct answers to these questions follow a dashed line after the frame. As you work through the book, use a folded paper or a card to cover the correct answer until you have written yours. And be sure you actually write each response, especially when the activity is coding CP/M-86 commands. Only by writing out the commands, and checking them carefully, can you get the most from this Self-Teaching Guide.

And don't worry! There's almost nothing you can do, apart from outright physical abuse, that can damage your system. Certainly there's no command you can enter that will hurt either CP/M-86 or the hardware. At the most, you can lose some data, and that's what this book and the Suggested Machine Exercises will help to prevent.

For the proper physical care of your equipment, see your manufacturer's recommendations.

Contents

CHAPTER ONE
Introduction to CP/M-86

The Control Program/Microcomputer-86 (CP/M-86) is a set of programs that runs the IBM Personal Computer. To be more specific, CP/M-86 enables you to control the operation of the microcomputer.

In this chapter we talk about the Personal Computer itself—the pieces of equipment that are required and optional when you're going to use CP/M-86. You will also learn how to start the computer with CP/M-86 and handle any problems you might encounter during the process.

When you have finished this chapter, you will be able to:

- Identify the major components of the Personal Computer.
- Start up CP/M-86.
- Interpret error messages that may result from starting up CP/M-86.
- Shut down CP/M-86.

PERSONAL COMPUTER COMPONENTS

The Personal Computer includes a system unit containing memory and at least one disk drive, a keyboard, some kind of monitor, and perhaps some other equipment as well. We'll look at these components before we talk about how to start up the computer.

1. The heart of the Personal Computer is contained in the *system unit*. Inside this unit is the microprocessor, which is the component containing the computer's logic and arithmetic circuits. It is the microprocessor that reads and executes programs. The system unit also contains memory—a set of circuits for storing programs and data while the microprocessor is working on them.

System Unit

One or two disk drives are built into the system unit. Our picture shows two disk drives, but your unit may have only one. The disk drives are used for storing programs and data so that the computer can copy them into memory when needed.

(a)   Name three components inside the system unit. _______________________

____

(b)   Which component contains the arithmetic and logic circuits?

____

(c)   Which component stores programs and data that the computer might want to copy?

____

(d)   Which component stores the programs and data that the computer is currently using?

____

— — — — — — — — — — — —

(a) microprocessor, memory, disk drives; (b) microprocessor; (c) disk drives; (d) memory

2.   The IBM Personal Computer that uses CP/M-86 must have between 32K and 1024K of memory. For any program to run on your computer, it must be stored in memory. (This includes the CP/M-86 programs.)

In computer terms, "K" refers to about 1000 bytes—actually 1024—and so 32K means 32,768 bytes. A *byte* is the amount of storage space required to store one character of data such as a letter, a digit, or a symbol. The letter K is an abbreviation for "kilobyte." Therefore your Personal Computer may hold anywhere from 32,768 to 1,048,576 characters of data, depending on how much memory it has.

(a) What term refers to the amount of storage needed to store one letter, such as

"B"? ____

(b) How would you specify that a memory has room for about 48,000 characters? ____

— — — — — — — — — —

(a) byte; (b) 48K

3. An IBM Personal Computer that uses CP/M–86 may have from one to four *disk drives*. At least one disk drive uses a 5¼-inch diameter "mini-floppy" disk. Each mini-floppy can hold up to 160K bytes of data on one side.

The mini-floppies are used for external storage of data. A vast amount of data can be stored this way because you can use numerous disks. They can be removed from the machine, when not in use, and other disks installed in their place. Thus, although each side of a mini-floppy can hold only 160K, you can store millions of bytes of data on several disks. The Personal Computer may have from one to four disk drives and each disk drive may be capable of reading one or two sides of a disk. Thus, the computer may have access to 160K (one side of one disk) to 1280K (both sides of four disks) of disk data at one time if all the drives are mini-floppy drives. (Hard disk drives, which you may also purchase for the Personal Computer, hold even more data.)

(a) Are disk drives used for memory or external storage?_______________

(b) How many disk drives can the Personal Computer that uses CP/M-86 have?

____

(c) How many bytes does one two-sided mini-floppy disk hold? ___________

(d) Which is true?

______ A. One computer system can have only four disks; so the maximum amount of external storage is 1280K bytes.

______ B. Only four disks at a time may be used, but a system may have hundreds of interchangeable disks, as well as other types of disk drives.

— — — — — — — — — —

(a) external storage; (b) at least one, and up to four; (c) 320K; (d) B

4.   The disk drives have alphabetical names within the CP/M–86 system. The first, or only, drive is called drive A. If your system unit has two disk drives, drive A is on the left as you face the system unit, and drive B is on the right. Drives C and D are usually found in a separate unit attached to the Personal Computer. If you have a hard disk unit, either in a separate cabinet or installed in the system unit in place of drive B, it will include drives C and D (and perhaps B also).

(a)   In the drawing below, label the disk drives with their names.

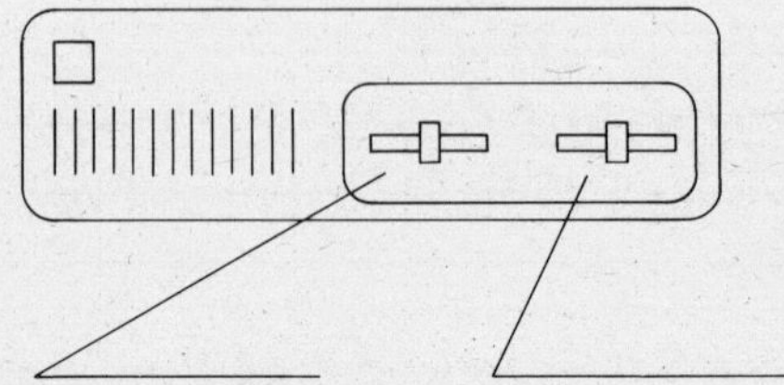

(b)   If a Personal Computer has four drives, what are they called?

____

— — — — — — — — — — — —

(a) A is on the left and B is on the right; (b) A, B, C, and D

5.   Attached to the system unit is a keyboard unit. This is the main means by which you communicate with the computer. You type commands on the keyboard, and CP/M-86 reads and obeys the commands.

Keyboard

Match these components with their functions:

_____(a) Disk drive

_____(b) Keyboard

_____(c) Memory

1. Stores programs and data currently being worked on.
2. Stores other programs and data.
3. Used to give commands to the computer.

—— —— —— —— —— —— ——

(a) 2; (b) 3; (c) 1

6. Your Personal Computer will have some type of monitor—a television-like device that the computer uses to communicate with you.

The standard monitor is a device that displays data in one color only (usually green) and thus is called a monochrome display. The monochrome display is good for displaying character data such as letters, numbers, and punctuation marks, but it is not so good for graphics and animation. Thus, the monochrome display is usually used in business settings, but not for action games.

IBM Monochrome Display

Instead of, or in addition to, the standard monochrome display, you may install a special Color/Graphics Monitor Adapter and hook up another monitor, either monochrome or color. The features you get (such as color graphics) depend on the monitor you select. In general, the more you pay, the more you get.

You can also use just a plain television set with the Color/Graphics Adapter, in either color or black and white. The television set has the advantage of displaying graphics and animation well (if it's a good set). But no TV set does a good job with character data; the resolution isn't good enough and they can display only 40 characters per line rather than the standard 80. Thus TV sets are frequently used for action games but not for business or scientific work.

Many home Personal Computers have *both* a monochrome display and a color TV set attached. Why do you suppose their owners hook up both types of devices?

____

____

— — — — — — — — — —

The monochrome display is for "serious" work such as personal accounting and word processing, while the color TV set is used for action games and graphic displays such as pie charts and bar graphs.

7. Your Personal Computer must have a system unit with at least one disk drive, a keyboard, and at least one monitor or TV set. It might also have some other units.

Most of the devices you can hook up to a computer fall into two categories: serial and parallel. The terms "serial" and "parallel" refer to the basic method used to transfer data between the device and the computer. Your personal computer has room in the system unit to add several circuit boards. (You may also hear these referred to as "cards.") The boards you add may increase your memory capacity, provide serial and parallel *ports* (these are plugs to hook up external devices), and provide other features as well. The number of serial and parallel ports you can add to your system is limited only by the ingenuity of the board designers (and your pocketbook, of course) since you can buy boards containing more than one part. The standard printer for the Personal Computer requires a parallel port; parallel ports are often called "printer ports" because most parallel devices are printers. You might also have a more sophisticated printer (a letter-quality printer) that attaches to a serial port.

Specify whether each of the following is a required or an optional component for CP/M-86.

(a) Letter-quality printer ____

(b) Standard printer ____

(c) System unit ____

(d) Monitor (or TV) ____

(e) Keyboard ____

— — — — — — — — — —

(a) optional; (b) optional; (c) required; (d) required; (e) required

8. CP/M-86 monitors a microcomputer system made up of various pieces of equipment, which is called *hardware*. CP/M-86 itself, however, is *software*; that is, CP/M-86 consists of programs and data, not equipment. CP/M-86 is an *operating system*; it is a system of programs that allow you to operate your computer. The software provided by CP/M-86 acts as an interface between the microprocessor and you. It also acts as an interface between the various hardware devices.

Which of the following are functions or features of CP/M-86?

_____ (a) Serves as a hardware device

_____ (b) Interfaces between pieces of hardware

_____ (c) Operating system

_____ (d) Software

— — — — — — — — — —

b; c; d

BOOTING *See Pg 13–8*

9. Let's assume now that you're ready to start your system. It has been set up, and all the necessary cables connected. The power is off. How do you get CP/M-86 up and running?

Step 1: You must use a disk containing the CP/M-86 system. For now, you will use the original system disk that came in the binder with the CP/M–86 manual. Later, we'll show you how to create and use other disks. Insert your system disk in drive A (you *must* use drive A for this, not any other drive). To do this, pull up the tab that covers the center of the disk

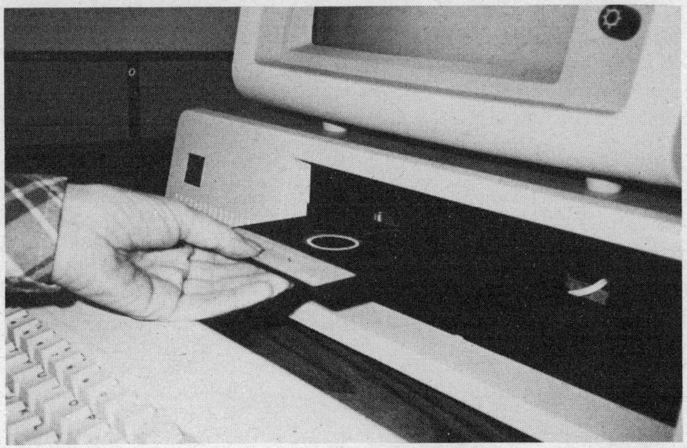

Installing a Disk in Drive A

slot. Remove the disk from its paper sleeve. Don't try to remove it from the permanent paper envelope, however; and don't touch the mylar parts that show through the envelope. With the label up, push the disk slowly into the disk unit as far as it will go. Then close the tab again, by pushing it down.

Step 2: Turn on your printer (if you have one). On the standard IBM printer, the on/off switch is a rocker switch on the right side at the back.

Step 3: Turn on your monitor or TV (if it has its own power switch; the standard monochrome display does not have one).

Step 4: Turn on the main power switch on the system unit. It's on the right at the back.

Actually, steps 2 through 4 may be done in any order, but step 1 must be done before step 4.

If all goes well, CP/M-86 will *boot*. This means that the CP/M-86 system is booted (or loaded) into the computer and it begins to operate. It can take quite a while (a minute or so); so be patient. It's testing memory to make sure everything is functioning properly.

(a) What must you do before you turn on the main power switch?

____

(b) What must be on the disk you boot from?

_______ A. BASIC.

_______ B. The CP/M-86 system.

_______ C. It must be blank.

(c) In which drive do you put the boot disk—the left-hand or right-hand one?

____

———————————————

(a) put disk in drive A; (b) B; (c) the left-hand one (if you try to boot from drive B, it won't work)

10.   A number of things can go wrong when you try to boot. For example, suppose you don't properly install a disk in drive A before turning on the power. The IBM Personal Computer BASIC system (built into the computer) will take over instead of CP/M-86. Here's what the screen would look like if a system disk is not properly installed in drive A:

```
The IBM Personal Computer Basic
Version C1.00 Copyright IBM Corp 1981
61404 Bytes free
Ok
```

This can happen if you don't close the tab properly, put the disk in upside down, or don't put any disk at all in the drive.

Suppose you install a disk in drive A properly, but the disk doesn't contain the proper CP/M-86 programs. You might get one of these messages:

```
Nonsystem disk or disk error
Replace and strike any key when ready
```

or

```
Disk boot failure
```

In the first case, you can put the disk in properly and then press any key. In the second case, you'll need to put the correct disk in drive A and reboot. (The next frame will show you how to reboot without using the main power switch.)

Suppose you try to boot CP/M-86 and get this message:

```
The IBM Personal Computer Basic
Version C1.00 Copyright IBM Corp 1981
61404 Bytes free
Ok
```

(a) What's wrong? ____

____

(b) How can you fix it? ____

____

Suppose you try to boot CP/M-86 and get this message:

```
Disk boot failure
```

(c) What's wrong? ____

____

(d) How can you fix it? ____

____

_ _ _ _ _ _ _ _ _ _ _ _ _

(a) you didn't put a disk in drive A properly; (b) install the disk properly and reboot; (c) the disk you tried to boot from does not contain the proper CP/M-86 programs for booting; (d) install a proper disk and reboot

11.   Sometimes you want to reboot when CP/M-86 is already working; that is, you want to restart CP/M-86 without using the power switch. You might do this to get rid of a bad program or command or to recover from a bad initial boot. When you reboot, CP/M-86 stops whatever it is doing and goes back to the beginning, but does not take the time to rerun the memory test.

You don't have to shut the power off to reboot. All you have to do is make sure the system disk is in drive A, then press three keys simultaneously: Ctrl, Alt, and Del. You can hold down Ctrl and Alt with your left hand and press Del with your right hand. The process is intentionally awkward to prevent your doing this accidentally and terminating a program you were using.

(a)   Rebooting interrupts (aborts) whatever the computer is currently doing. True or false? ____

(b)   What keys are used in rebooting?___________________________________

(c)   In what order must they be pressed?________________________________

— — — — — — — — — — —

(a) true; (b) Ctrl, Alt, Del; (c) all together

12.   When the system has been booted properly, you'll see the following information on your screen.

```
CP/M–86 Bootstrap Loader n.n
Reading Track 0 1 2 3 4

CP/M–86 for the IBM Personal Computer.
Version n.n
Copyright year, Digital Research Inc.

Hardware Supported :
                              Diskette(s)    :   n
                                Printer(s)   :   n
                            Serial Port(s)   :   n
                            Memory (Kb)      :   nnn
A>_


            |U=00|02/10/82|00:00:00|
```

We'll analyze these messages line by line. The first line indicates that the program that boots the CP/M-86 system is working. The name of this program is the CP/M-86 Bootstrap Loader. The n.n at the end of the line is the version number of this program. The second line is displayed by the Bootstrap Loader. It gives you a progress report on reading the system from the disk tracks. You can watch the numbers pop up as you hear the disk drive working.

After the CP/M-86 system has been put into memory, it takes over the computer. Then you see the next set of lines. The fourth line tells you the name of the program, the fifth line tells you its version number, and the sixth line reminds you that Digital Research, Inc., developed the program and holds the copyright. You are not free to make copies of this program, except for your own use on your own Personal Computer.

CP/M-86 then does a survey of the hardware it "sees" and lists the results: the number of disk drives, the number of devices hooked up to printer (parallel) ports, the number of devices hooked up to serial ports, and the amount of memory, expressed in kilobytes.

Now look at the line after "Memory (Kb): nnn". It looks like this:

```
A>_
```


The A> is the CP/M-86 command prompt. It tells you that the CP/M-86 system is ready to receive your command. You'll learn more about the command prompt in the next chapter.

At the bottom of the screen is a status line. (See the sample screen below.) It tells you your user number, the date, and the time. (When you boot, the date and time will be wrong.) You will learn what a user number is, how these figures are used by CP/M-86, and how you can change them, later in this book.

Here is the boot screen from a very early version of CP/M-86.

```
CP/M–86 Bootstrap Loader 1.0
Reading Track 0 1 2 3 4

CP/M–86 for the IBM Personal Computer.
Version 1.0
Copyright 1982, Digital Research Inc.

Hardware Supported  :
                                Diskette(s)    :   2
                                 Printer(s)    :   1
                              Serial Port(s)   :   0
                                Memory (Kb)    :   064
A>_

              0 |U=00|02/10/82|00:00:08|
```

(a) What version of the Bootstrap Loader was being used? _________________

(b) Which program read tracks 0 through 4 from the disk?_________________

(c) How many disk drives does this system have? _________________

(d) How much memory space does this system have?_____ bytes

(e) Which of the following is the CP/M-86 command prompt?

    _____ A. U=00

    _____ B. Hardware Supported:

    _____ C. A>

(f) What does the command prompt tell you?

    _____ A. CP/M-86 is ready to receive a command.

    _____ B. CP/M-86 is busy processing a command.

    _____ C. CP/M-86 has processed n commands since booting.

(g) What date does CP/M-86 think it is? _________________

———————————

(a) 1.0; (b) the Bootstrap Loader; (c) 2; (d) 64K; (e) C; (f) A; (g) 02/10/82 (If you have a later version of CP/M-86, your initial screen may look different from this example.)

13.   If you have trouble remembering the boot procedure later on, you can look it up. Either come back to this book or use your IBM CP/M-86 reference manual.

If you encounter a message you don't understand, you can look it up in your CP/M-86 manual. In the back is an appendix explaining the various CP/M-86 messages. It is organized into two sections. The first section explains messages that appear in the status line at the bottom of the screen. That section is organized into two subsections: disk messages and printer messages. So if you get a message on the status line (usually accompanied by an electronic beep from the computer), look it up under the disk or printer section. Disk messages start with "Disk d:", where d is the name of the drive. Printer messages start with "Printer n:", where n is the number of the printer.

The second section of the appendix contains messages in response to commands. These messages are displayed not on the status line but right after the command. Here is an example:

```
A>TOD 5/10
Invalid Date and Time Format
Please retry using:
  TOD MM/DD/YY HH:MM:SS
A>_
```

Here we tried to change the date to 5/10, but we used the wrong format for the TOD ("time of day") command. The error message tells us that and indicates the correct format.

Find the Messages appendix in your CP/M-86 reference manual and use it to answer the following questions.

(a)   Suppose the following message appears on your status line.

```
Printer 0: Busy
```

What should you do?

_______ A.   Wait until the printer is not busy.

_______ B.   Check the cables between the printer and the system unit.

_______ C.   Turn the printer off and then on again.

(b) Suppose the following message appears on your status line.

```
Disk A: Controller failed
```

What should you do?

____ A. Try again.

____ B. Try another disk in drive A.

____ C. Try the same disk in drive B.

———————————————

(a) B; (b) A

14. How do you shut the system down again? Turn off the main power switch. You can remove the disks either before or after you shut it down. Store your disks carefully. They're not overly fragile, but they're not hardy either. They don't like smoke, dust, dirt, fingerprints, liquids, scratches, or magnetism. It's best to keep them in their paper sleeves and inside another container—a box or a binder.

(a) True or false? You must remove the disks before you shut off the system

unit. ______

(b) True or false? Floppy disks need to be handled and stored carefully.

______

———————————————

(a) false—they can be removed either before or after the power is shut off; (b) true

Now you have learned what hardware components are required by CP/M-86, how to start up (boot) CP/M-86, and how to shut it down again.

Chapter One Self-Test

This Self-Test will help you determine if you have mastered the objectives of this chapter. Answer each question to the best of your ability, then check your answers in the answer key at the end of the test.

1. Which of the following are required components of a Personal Computer under CP/M-86?

    _____ a. Memory

    _____ b. Disk drive(s)

    _____ c. Parallel ports

    _____ d. Monitor or TV

    _____ e. Serial ports

    _____ f. Printer

    _____ g. Keyboard

2. Which drive do you boot from? _____ Which side is that on? _________

3. Put the following boot steps in order.

    _____ a. Turn on main power switch on system unit.

    _____ b. Put proper disk in boot drive.

    _____ c. Turn on printer and monitor.

4. Suppose you try to boot and get this message:

   ```
   Nonsystem disk or disk error
   Replace and strike any key when ready
   ```

    a. What's wrong? ____

    b. How can you fix it? _____________________________________

    ____

5. Which keys are used to reboot?_____________________________________

Self-Test Answer Key

Compare your answers to the Self-Test with the correct answers given below. If all your answers are correct, you are ready to go on to the next chapter. If you missed any questions, you may find it helpful to review the appropriate frames before going on.

1. a, b, d, g

2. A, left

3. The important thing is to do step b before step a.

4. a. Something's wrong with the disk you're booting from.
   b. Install a good boot disk and strike any key.

5. Ctrl, Alt, Del

Suggested Machine Exercise

Each chapter in this book ends with a suggested machine exercise. If you have your Personal Computer and CP/M-86 disk, we strongly recommend that you work these exercises. This is the best way to become comfortable with CP/M-86.

If you don't know how to boot your system, this first exercise is vital because every other exercise in this book starts by booting.

Your system must be set up before you work this exercise. That is, it must be out of the box, and all the cables must be hooked up properly. If your system has not yet been set up, follow the directions in your Guide to Operations. Then work the exercise below.

What You Should Do	*What the Computer Will Do*

1. Practice booting the system
  a. Put system disk in drive A.
  b. Turn on monitor and any other peripheral devices.
  c. Turn on main power switch on system unit.
(See frames 9 and 11.)
	Nothing at first. Then beep. Then display cursor. Then read from drive A and begin displaying initial screen. *Note:* If this doesn't happen, shut off the main power. Wait 5 minutes (important!) and try again. If it still doesn't work, get help.

2. Practice rebooting. a. Hold down Ctrl and Alt and press Del. (See frame 11.)	Reboot from the disk in drive A. The initial screen will be redisplayed.

3. Shut down the system.
  a. Turn off the main power switch.
  b. Turn off any peripheral units.
  c. Remove the system disk and store it properly.
(See frame 14.)
	Lights will go out. Monitor screen will darken.

4. Try a few "bad" boots to see what the messages are like. (Don't worry, you won't hurt the computer.)
  a. Turn the power on with no disk in drive A.
  b. Shut it down again.
  c. Put a blank disk in drive A and turn the power on.
(See frame 10.)
	Boot with BASIC instead of CP/M-86.
	
	Shut down.
	Display an error message.

5.	Practice booting and rebooting several times, until you feel comfortable with the process.	If at any time the computer does not respond, TURN IT OFF and let it rest 5 minutes before proceeding.
6.	Shut down the system and go on to Chapter Two.	

CHAPTER TWO

The CP/M-86 Components

You've seen the hardware side of CP/M-86. Now it's time to look at the software side. In this chapter, you'll learn what programs CP/M-86 includes. You'll also learn how CP/M-86 organizes and controls data on disks and how CP/M-86 responds to your commands.

When you have finished this chapter, you will be able to:

- Identify the functions of the major parts of the CP/M-86 system.
- Recognize valid file identifiers.
- Select a default disk drive.
- Interpret error messages that may result from drive selection.

THE CP/M-86 PROGRAMS

We have said several times that CP/M-86 is a *set* of programs. In the frames that follow, we'll overview the major CP/M-86 programs.

1.　One major CP/M-86 program is the Basic Input/Output System (BIOS). BIOS is a set of functions that controls all input and output (I/O) between memory and the other devices. When a program wants to write data to the printer or read data from the keyboard (for example), the program calls on BIOS to actually handle the read or write function.

(a)　What does BIOS stand for? _______________________________________

(b)　What does BIOS do?

_______ A.　Identifies when the printer runs out of paper.

_______ B.　Controls I/O functions.

_______ C.　Prevents division by zero.

— — — — — — — — — — —

(a) Basic Input/Output System; (b) B

2. Another CP/M-86 program is called Basic Disk Operating System (BDOS). It controls the organization of data on the disks.

Data on disks is organized in files. A file is a set of related data. For example, your office might have a payroll file that contains the payroll information for all your company's employees. The file, in turn, contains records. For the payroll file there would be one record for each employee containing the employee's name, address, wage rate, tax rate, and so forth.

The payroll file is an example of a data file. Another type of file you will have is a program file, which contains all the commands that make up one computer program. Each command is a record.

One disk may contain many files. It's not unusual to have more than 50 files on one disk. BDOS keeps track of all files on the disk.

(a) What is the basic function of BDOS? ___________________________

____

(b) Which of the following statements is true?

_____ A. A disk contains records, which contain files.

_____ B. A disk contains files, which contain records.

— — — — — — — — — —

(a) organize data on disks; (b) B

3. Every disk file must have a name. BDOS keeps a file *directory* on each disk. The directory shows all the file names and their exact locations on the disk.

Every time you add a new file to a disk BDOS does the following:

* Checks the directory to make sure there is no file with the same name.
* Checks the directory to make sure there is room for the file.
* Updates the directory with an entry for the new file.

(a) What CP/M-86 program maintains the disk directory? _______________

(b) What information does the disk directory contain?

____

____

— — — — — — — — — —

(a) BDOS; (b) file name and file location

4. The preceding frames have discussed the BIOS and BDOS programs. Another major set of programs is the *console command processor* (CCP). This is the part you will use directly. The CCP reads whatever you type on the keyboard and processes the commands you give it. You can enter commands to list a directory or erase a file, and the CCP will process the command and do as you ask. You can request processing external to the CCP, and the CCP will handle the request and then return to you. All your commands at the keyboard are handled through the console command processor of CP/M-86.

(a) What is the name of the console command processor? ________________

(b) Can you interact with CP/M-86 without using the command processor?

      _______ If so, how? ____

— — — — — — — — — — —

(a) CCP; (b) no

5. The CCP program contains several routines for functions that you will use all the time. You will learn how to use the functions in Chapter Four, but we'll overview them here:

- DIR displays the directory of the files on a disk.
- ERA erases a file from a disk.
- TYPE displays a file.
- REN renames a file.
- USER displays and changes the user number.

Because these functions are part of the console command processor, they're always available to you whenever you see the CP/M-86 command prompt. The commands that you type to use them (DIR, ERA, etc.) are called the built-in commands.

(a) What major CP/M-86 program processes the built-in commands?

____

(b) If your computer is on but you haven't booted CP/M-86 into memory, would

    the built-in commands work? ____

    Why? ____

— — — — — — — — — —

(a) CCP; (b) no, because they're part of CP/M-86

6. The other CP/M-86 programs you are studying in this section, such as BIOS and BDOS, are also built into the CP/M-86 package. Whenever CP/M-86 is running on your system, they are automatically stored in memory and are available to CP/M-86. However, you have no commands to use them. They are called only by other programs. For example, the CCP uses BIOS to communicate with your keyboard.

Even though they are built-in programs, they have no matching built-in commands.

Match the functions below with their characteristics.

_____(a) CCP, BIOS,   1. Internal commands
        BDOS   2. Always available when CP/M-86 is running
_____(b) DIR, ERA, TYPE

— — — — — — — — — —

(a) 2; (b) 1, 2

7. Any program that is not built-in is called a *transient* program. The term "transient" refers to the fact that the program is loaded into main memory only when it is needed. A transient program is kept in a file on disk. Its filename becomes the command that you type if you want to use the program.

Your system disk contains several transient programs provided as part of CP/M-86. You might also acquire transient programs from other sources or write your own.

There are only a few built-in commands, but you can have as many transient commands as you can fit files on your disks.

Match the program types on the left with their descriptions on the right.

_____(a) Built-in program   1. Stored in memory only when needed
                        2. Always in memory when CP/M-86 is
_____(b) Transient program   running
                        3. Can be written by users
                        4. Can be bought from other sources and
                          added to system
                        5. Part of CP/M-86 package from IBM

— — — — — — — — — —

(a) 2, 5; (b) 1, 3, 4, 5

8. The built-in programs are always in memory whenever CP/M-86 is running. A transient program must be loaded into memory from disk each time it is used.

Which type of programs do you think would start up faster? _______________

Why? ____

— — — — — — — — — —

built-in programs; because there's no loading time

9. (a) Which CP/M-86 program contains the built-in commands? __________

    (b) A program that's loaded from disk into memory each time it's used is

        called ____

    (c) Which type of program starts faster? _______________________________

— — — — — — — — — —

(a) CCP; (b) a transient program; (c) built-in

Now you know that CP/M-86 is an operating system, made up of BIOS, BDOS, the CCP, and a variety of transient programs.

Now we're going to look more closely at some other components that you'll be using with CP/M-86: the disk drives, the disks, and the files that reside on the disks.

THE DEFAULT DRIVE

10. When the system is ready to receive a command, the CCP displays a message like this:

```
A>_
```

The message (called a "prompt") tells you two things: the command processor is ready to receive a command, and the default disk drive is A. The default drive is the disk drive where CP/M-86 will look for programs and data files. For example, if A is the default drive and you enter the command STAT SOURCE1, CP/M-86 will look on drive A for the STAT program as well as the SOURCE1 file.

You can change the default drive by entering the desired drive name followed by a colon. If you type this:

```
B:
```

and press Enter, the command processor responds with this:

```
B>_
```

Now drive B is the default drive, and the command processor is ready for another command.

(a)   Given the prompt below, which drive is the default drive? _______________

```
B>_
```

(b)   Suppose your Personal Computer has two drives. Write a command to make the other drive the default drive. B> _______________________________

(c)   When CP/M-86 is started, which drive becomes the default?_______________

— — — — — — — — — — —

(a) drive B
(b) A:
(c) drive A

11.   The colon is a critical part of drive selection. If you enter a drive name without the colon, the CCP doesn't know you want to select a drive. It thinks you want to run a program of that name. If it can't find any program with that name, you'll get a message like this:

```
B?

A>_
```

The prompt you get always indicates the default drive. Because the CP/M-86 system didn't recognize B as a drive name, the A drive remained the default drive.

If you enter an invalid drive name, you'll get an error message, as in this interaction:

```
A>H:
H:?

A>_
```

Notice that a command prompt (A>) follows the error message (H:?). CP/M-86 has rejected the previous command and is waiting for another one. You do not have to erase the incorrect command. Just go ahead and enter a correct one. For each example below, tell what happened.

(a)   A>B:
          B>_

___

(b)   A>J:
          J:?

          A>_

___

(c)   A>B
          B?

          A>_

___

— — — — — — — — — —

(a) drive B was selected; (b) there is no J drive; (c) the colon was omitted and drive A remains selected; also, no program named B exists on drive A

DISKS

12.   Each side of each disk is divided into 40 tracks with eight sectors, as you can see here. The *tracks* are concentric rings. The *sectors* form wedges that intersect with the tracks. You can see that sector 20, track 7, could be used to refer to a specific part of the disk. (You won't have to do this, but CP/M-86 does when it locates files or data.) Sometimes when CP/M-86 finds something physically wrong with a disk, it tells you the track or sector involved.

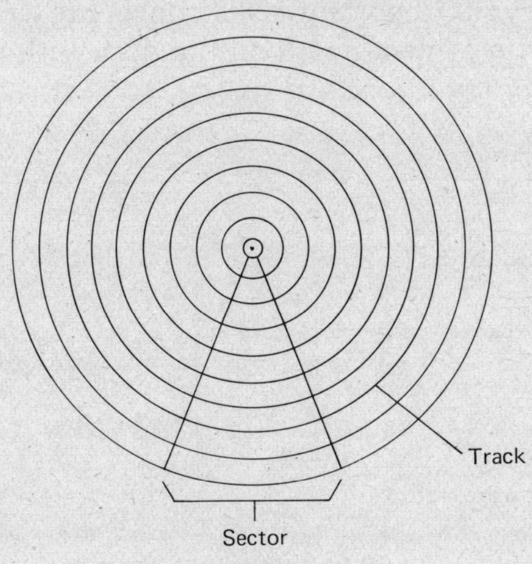

Tracks and Sectors

The track nearest the outside edge is track 0, and the next is track 1. The disk directory is kept in the first part of track 0. The rest of the disk is available to store programs and data files. The CP/M-86 system programs BDOS, BIOS, and CCP are kept on tracks 0 through 4, if they are on the disk, leaving only 35 tracks (on a single-sided disk) for your programs and files. (If the system programs are not on the disk, you can't use it for booting, but you could use it in drive B.)

(a)   What is the difference between a track and a sector? _________________

____

(b)   Which track contains the disk directory? ________________________

____

(c)   On a single-sided system disk, how many tracks are available for your programs and data files? ____

— — — — — — — — — — — —

(a) tracks are concentric rings and sectors are wedges; (b) track zero; (c) 35

13. You can protect your important disks from being written on. You do this by covering over the write protect notch on the disk with a piece of tape.

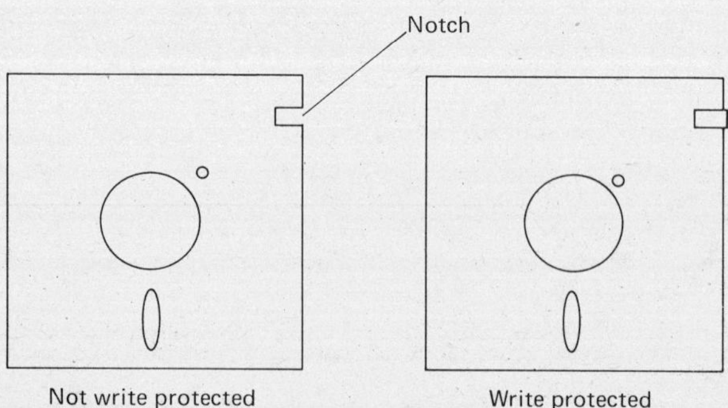

Once a disk has been write protected, it cannot be written on unless you remove the tape. You can read any file on the disk, but you can't add new files or change any files already there. Because you can't write on the directory, you can't erase or rename files either.

If you buy a program for your system, you may find that it is permanently write protected by virtue of having no notch.

Match each disk status with its allowable operations.

_____(a) Write protected

_____(b) Not write protected

1. Read files
2. Erase files
3. Change files
4. Rename files
5. Write new files

Label each of the following as true or false.

(c) Every 5¼ inch floppy disk has a write protect notch._________________

(d) Once a disk has been write protected, it can never be written on.________

— — — — — — — — — — — —

(a) 1; (b) 1, 2, 3, 4, 5; (c) false; (d) false—the write protection can be removed

14. Another way to protect a disk is to give it read-only (R/O) status while you're using it. Read-only status means that you cannot write on the disk.

This is only temporary protection, as it applies only until the disk is removed from the drive (or until you reboot).

Whenever you boot, all disks already in the computer are given read-write (R/W) status. (They will still be write-protected if their notches are taped over.) If you change the disk in a drive, the new disk automatically receives read-only status. To clear the R/O status, type Ctrl-C after you have changed the disk. To type this, you hold down the Ctrl (Control) key and press the C key. (You could also reboot, but that's not necessary.) After Ctrl-C (or reboot), the new disk will have R/W status.

You can also assign R/O status to a disk using the STAT command, which you will study in Chapter Six. Even if you assign R/O status this way, Ctrl-C or a reboot will give all disks R/W status.

(a)   Which of the following statements is true?

_____ A.   R/O protection is more permanent than the write-protect notch.

_____ B.   R/O protection is less permanent than the write-protect notch.

Suppose you have disks in drives A and B. The power is off.

(b)   After you boot the system, what status does disk A have?_____________

(c)   What status does disk B have? _______________________________________

(d)   Suppose you change the disk in drive B. What status does the new disk

have? ____

(e)   How can you change its status? _______________________________________

— — — — — — — — — —

(a) B; (b) R/W; (c) R/W; (d) R/O; (e) press Ctrl-C or reboot

15.   It's time to talk about a common (and detested) message from CP/M-86:

    BDOS ERROR ON d:

This tells you that the BDOS program cannot access the disk in drive d: (which can be A: B: C: or D:) for some reason. The message usually includes the reason. For example:

    BDOS ERROR ON B: R/O

This message means you tried to write on a disk with R/O status.

When you get the BDOS ERROR message, the system waits for you to respond. All you have to do is strike any key. Then enter a Ctrl-C to give the disk R/W status if you want.

Suppose you get this message:

    BDOS ERROR ON A: R/O_

(a)   What is wrong? ____

(b)   How do you respond to this message? _________________________________

— — — — — — — — — —

(a) you tried to write on a disk with R/O status; (b) strike any key and then enter Ctrl-C if you want to give the disk R/W status

FILES

16.   A *file* on a disk is a finite set of information. It may be a program, data, a letter, or a report. A file is anything you have called a file and stored on disk.

Every file on a disk has a unique identifier with up to three parts. You will also see the file identifier called the file specifier or the filespec. Here's an example of a file identifier:

     A:CHAPTER1.PRN

Let's look at the parts of this identifier separately.

The first part is the drivename. This part of the file identifier may vary, depending on which drive holds the disk. It's not a *permanent* part of the file identifier. If used, it's followed by a colon.

The second part is the filename. It has from one to eight characters and must start with a letter. Letters or numbers can be used for the other characters. Avoid special characters such as −, # and ; some of them are illegal.

The third part is the filetype. It has from zero to three characters (either letters or numbers). Not every file needs a filetype. But if one is used, it is separated from the filename by a period.

If you type a filename longer than eight characters or a filetype longer than three characters, CP/M-86 truncates (chops off) the extra characters. Thus, WEDNESDAYS.MENUS will be read as WEDNESDA.MEN.

Indicate if each name below is a valid CP/M-86 file identifier. If not, state why it is invalid.

(a) A:FILE6

     valid _____ invalid _______________________________

(b) FILE6.SIX

     valid _____ invalid _______________________________

(c) 6FILE.SIX

     valid _____ invalid _______________________________

(d) FILESIXTEEN

     valid _____ invalid _______________________________

(e) A

     valid _____ invalid _______________________________

— — — — — — — — — — —

(a) valid; (b) valid; (c) invalid, doesn't begin with a letter; (d) this is valid but will be read as FILESIXT; (e) valid (but could be confused with drive A:)

17. When you create a new file, you can make up the filename and filetype. But CP/M-86 recognizes certain filetypes and may treat them differently. Here are a few of the many CP/M-86 standard filetypes:

> SUB—a file containing CP/M-86 commands
> CMD—a transient program
> $$$—a temporary file

Many files will have filetypes needed by your transient programs. You may have an inventory program that will only work on a file with the filetype INV. You may have a mailing label program that creates a file with the filetype LAB. Many of your file identifiers will have no filetypes because they aren't needed for any special reason.

Indicate if each filetype is valid or invalid. If it is invalid, tell why:

(a) COM

   valid _____ invalid ____

(b) PRACTICE

   valid _____ invalid ____

(c) DOC

   valid _____ invalid ____

(d) 6X

   valid _____ invalid ____

— — — — — — — — — — —

(a) valid; (b) valid but will be read as PRA; (c) valid; (d) valid

18. Each combination of filename and filetype on a disk must be unique. That means you may have several files named TEXT1 on a disk if each has a different filetype. You may also have several files with the same filetype as long as each has a different filename. The drivename will be the same for each file on the same disk. You can use the same filename-filetype combination on many different disks because you'll never have two disks on the same disk drive at once.

Which of the sets of complete file identifiers below represent unique names?

____(a)	A:TEXT1.DOC A:TEXT1.BAK A:TEXT1	____(c)	A:TEXT3.DOC B:TEXT3.DOC B:TEXT3.BAK
____(b)	A:TEXT2.DOC A:TEXT2 A:TEXT2	____(d)	B:TEXT4.DOC B:TEXT3.DOC A:TEXT4.DOC

— — — — — — — — — —

a, c, d

19. Every file has two attributes: read-write and directory. Within the read-write attribute are two possible statuses: R/O (read-only) and R/W (read-write). This attribute controls whether or not you can write on the file. This is very much like the R/W and R/O statuses for disks, except it's much more permanent. The file read-write status is stored in the file's directory entry, and the only way you can change it is with the STAT command.

The directory attribute controls whether or not the file will be displayed in a directory listing. The directory attribute has two possible statuses: DIR (directory) and SYS (system). A SYS file does not show up in a regular directory listing. We usually assign SYS status to those program files that we put on every disk; we don't need them in the directory listing because we know they're there. You can also get a directory of the system files for a disk; DIR files will not show up on that listing. The STAT command is used to assign DIR or SYS status to a file.

Suppose FILEA has R/O and SYS status.

(a) Can you write on FILEA? ____

(b) Can you erase it? ____

(c) Will it show up in a regular directory listing for the disk?_______________

Suppose FILEB has R/W and DIR status.

(d) Can you write on FILEB? ____

(e) Can you erase it? ____

(f) Will it show up in a regular directory listing for the disk?_______________

(g) What command can be used to give FILEB R/O and SYS status?

____

Suppose you get this message:

```
BDOS ERROR ON B: FILE R/O
```

(h) What do you suppose is wrong? _______________________________

(i) How do you respond to this message? _______________________________

(j) After your response, what read/write status will the file have?_________

— — — — — — — — — —

(a) no; (b) no; (c) no; (d) yes; (e) yes; (f) yes; (g) STAT; (h) you tried to write on an R/O file; (i) press any key; (j) still R/O

Chapter Two Self-Test

This Self-Test will help you determine if you have mastered the objectives of this chapter. Answer each question to the best of your ability, then check your answers in the answer key at the end of the test.

1. Identify the CP/M-86 program that performs each function below:

    a. Interprets keyboard entries. _______________________________

    b. Performs file management. _______________________________

    c. Handles input and output requests. _______________________________

2. Suppose your screen shows this prompt:

    ```
    A>_
    ```

    a. What is the default drive? _______________________________

    b. Write a command to switch to drive B. _______________________________

    c. What does it mean if the CCP responds

    ```
    B?
    A>_
    ```

3. Which of the complete file identifiers below represents a file of type COM, name STEST, on drive A?

   _____ a. A.COM.STEST

   _____ b. A.STEST.COM

   _____ c. A:STEST:COM

   _____ d. A:STEST.COM

4. Match.

   _____ a. Built-in programs

   _____ b. Transient programs

   (1) Reside in memory after CP/M-86 is booted
   (2) Reside on disk after CP/M-86 is booted
   (3) Start faster
   (4) Contained in the CCP
   (5) More can be written or purchased

5. How can you protect a valuable disk from being accidentally overwritten or erased?

   ____

   ____

6. Suppose you change the disk in drive B.

   a. What status will the new disk have? _______________________

   b. How can you change that status? _______________________

7. Suppose you boot with disks in drive A and B.

   a. What status will disk B have? _______________________

   b. How can you change that status? _______________________

8. What attributes can a file have?

   _____ a. DIR or SYS

   _____ b. PGM or DAT

   _____ c. R/O or R/W

   _____ d. ASC or BIN

9. What files will show up in a regular directory listing of a disk?

   _____ a. All files except CP/M-86 programs.

   _____ b. All files on the disk.

   _____ c. All DIR files on the disk.

   _____ d. All SYS files on the disk.

10. Suppose you get this message:

    BDOS ERROR ON B: R/O

    a. What's wrong? _______________________________________

    b. How do you respond to this message?

    ____

Self-Test Answer Key

Compare your answers to the Self-Test with the correct answers given below. If all your answers are correct, you are ready to go on to the next chapter. If you missed any questions, you may find it helpful to review the appropriate frames before going on.

1. a. The CCP
    b. BDOS
    c. BIOS

2. a. Drive A
    b. B:
    c. You entered B without the colon.

3. d

4. a. 1,3,4
    b. 2,5

5. Put tape over the write protect notch.

6. a. R/O
    b. Ctrl-C or reboot

7. a. R/W
    b. STAT command

8. a and c

9. c

10. a. You tried to write on an R/O disk.
    b. Press any key.

Suggested Machine Exercise

In this exercise, you will practice selecting the default drive if you have more than one drive. (If not, skip this exercise and go on to Chapter Three.)

What You Should Do	*What the Computer Will Do*
1. Boot the system. (Refer to the Chapter One machine exercise if you forget how.)	Display the initial screen.

2. Install *any* disk in drive B.
    a. Open the tab for drive B.
    b. Slide the disk in, label side up.
    c. Close the tab.
	Nothing

3. Switch to drive B.
    a. Type the letter B (upper- or lowercase) followed by a colon (:).
    b. Your command line should look like this:
 	
        A>B:
 	
    or this:
 	
        A>b:
 	
    c. Press Enter (↵).
(See frames 10 and 11.)
	Display the command prompt for the B drive: B>

4. Switch back to drive A again.
    a. Type the letter A (upper- or lowercase) followed by a colon (:).
    b. Your command line should look like this:
 	
        B>A:
 	
    or this:
 	
        B>a:
 	
    c. Press Enter (↵)
(See frames 10 and 11.)
	Display the command prompt for the A drive: A>

5.	Switch back and forth a few more times until you're comfortable with the process.	
6.	Now try to get some error messages. a. Try switching to drive X. b. Type B *without* the colon and press Enter. (See frame 11.)	Display this message: X:? Display this message: B?
7.	Continue experimenting with drive selection until you feel completely comfortable with it. Then shut down your system and go on to Chapter Three.	

CHAPTER THREE
Typing CP/M-86 Commands

You use CP/M-86 programs by typing and entering commands. A typical command might be

    ERA JOHNSON.LET

This command asks CP/M-86 to erase the disk file named JOHNSON.LET. There are many commands corresponding to the various CP/M-86 built-in and transient programs. You'll be learning the command details in later chapters. In this chapter, we will cover the general format of all CP/M-86 commands, what happens when a CP/M-86 command is entered, and some special keys you can use when typing CP/M-86 commands.

When you complete your study of this chapter, you will be able to:

- Identify the location of special keys on the Personal Computer keyboard.
- Identify the control keys that invoke major CP/M-86 control functions.
- Write a basic CP/M-86 command involving a program and a file.
- Write CP/M-86 commands for programs that are not on the default drive.
- Write CP/M-86 commands for files that are not on the default drive.
- Briefly describe what happens after a CP/M-86 command is entered.
- Interpret error messages resulting from CP/M-86 commands.

SPECIAL KEYS

Figure 3.1 shows the layout of the Personal Computer keyboard. We will use it in the following frames.

Figure 3.1   The Keyboard

1. Your Personal Computer keyboard contains all the keys of a traditional typewriter and many special keys as well.

The letter and number keys are laid out just like a standard typewriter. Other keys are somewhat different. If you know touch typing, you will need a little practice to adapt to this keyboard. One major difference is that any of these keys will repeat if held down.

Each letter key has an upper- and a lowercase. The uppercase—A CAPITAL LETTER—is reached by holding down a Shift key while hitting the letter key. There are two Shift keys on the keyboard, in standard typewriter positions for such keys. Each one is labeled with this symbol: ⇧.

To the right of the space bar is the CapsLock key. It is like a toggle switch; that is, push it once and shift lock is on; push it again and the shift is unlocked. You don't have to hold it down to keep it on. When CapsLock is on, all letters will type in uppercase. Numbers and other characters are not affected. The symbols over the number keys are typed by holding down a Shift key while striking the appropriate character key.

Be careful about the letter L and the number 1. The computer will not read a lowercase L as a one, even in something as "obvious" as 1985. You must use the number key in the top row for the number one. The same is true for the letter O and the number 0.

(a)   Which key is immediately to the left of the right-hand Shift key? (Choose one.)

______   A.   ?/

______   B.   ? Home

______   C.   }]

______   D.   + =

(b)   Which key is immediately to the left of the left-hand Shift key? (Choose one.)

   _____ A.   F4

   _____ B.   Ctrl

   _____ C.   F8

   _____ D.   Alt

(c)   On the Personal Computer keyboard, the letter and number keys have a much better layout than on a standard typewriter. True or false? _________

(d)   Which of the following is true?

   _____ A.   The CapsLock key causes all letters to be uppercase, but not numbers.
   _____ B.   The CapsLock key causes both letters and numbers to be shifted to uppercase.

(e)   Which of the following is true?

   _____ A.   To use CapsLock, you have to hold it down while you type the letters, just like a Shift key.
   _____ B.   CapsLock is turned on when you press the key once and stays on until you press it again.

(f)   Which of the following is true?

   _____ A.   The computer will interpret the letter L as either a letter or a number, whichever is more appropriate.
   _____ B.   You must be careful to use the number key and not the lowercase letter L to type the number one.

_ _ _ _ _ _ _ _ _ _ _ _

(a) A; (b) C; (c) false—they have the same layout as a standard keyboard; (d) A; (e) B; (f) B

2.   Computer programs tend to use more symbols than regular text, so your keyboard has more symbols than a regular typewriter.

   To the right of the left-hand Shift key is a key containing \ and 1.

   The comma key has < over it and the period key has > over it.

These will take some time to learn if you are used to commas and periods in both the uppercase and lowercase positions.

   Above the right-hand Shift key is a key containing ` and ˜. Next to the P are two keys containing [{ and] }. The standard typewriter symbols, such as ; @ and +, are also available in their usual positions.

Which of the following symbols are available on the Personal Computer keyboard?

_____ (a) ÷	_____ (d)]	_____ (g) Σ
_____ (b) {	_____ (e) =	_____ (h) ˜
_____ (c) ℏ	_____ (f) @	_____ (i) ǀ

— — — — — — — — — —

b, d, e, f, h, i

3. Whenever you want to enter any data, such as the date, you type the data, then hit the Enter key, which looks like this:

It is in the same position that the CARRIAGE RETURN key is in on most electric typewriters, where you can hit it with the little finger of your right hand. CP/M-86 will not read data in most cases until you hit the Enter key.

(a)   When this book or one of your other manuals tells you to "enter" something, what two steps are involved?____

____

(b)   CP/M-86 reads each character as you type it. True or false?_______________

(c)   What symbol is on the Enter key?____

— — — — — — — — — —

(a) type the data, hit Enter; (b) false—it waits until you press Enter; (c)

4. The keyboard has several keys labeled with arrows. You have already learned to identify the Enter key, which has this symbol: ⏎ and the Shift keys, which have this symbol: ⇧.

Above the Enter key is the backspace key, which has this symbol: ←.

Next to the Q is the tab key, which has this symbol: ⇄. The lowercase is the forward tab represented by →|. The uppercase doesn't do anything under CP/M-86, although it might with other programs you use.

Match the symbols with their meanings.

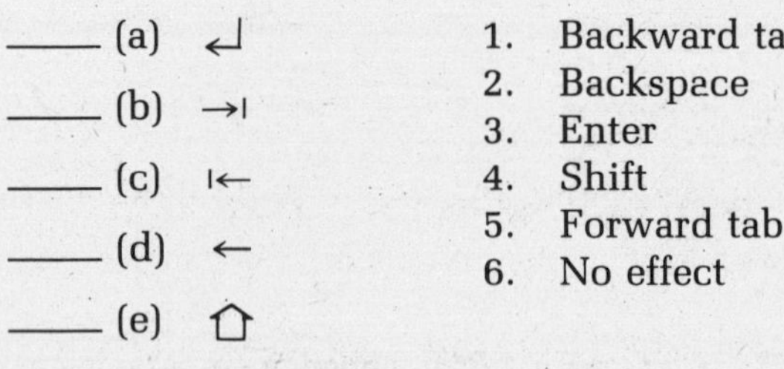

____ (a) ⏎	1.	Backward tab
____ (b) →|	2.	Backspace
	3.	Enter
____ (c) |←	4.	Shift
	5.	Forward tab
____ (d) ←	6.	No effect
____ (e) ⇧		

— — — — — — — — — —

(a) 3; (b) 5; (c) 6; (d) 2; (e) 4

5. To the right of the standard keyboard is the numeric keypad. If you are accustomed to a 10-key calculator, you may prefer to use the numeric keypad to enter numeric data. The numeric keypad consists of the digits 0 to 9, a decimal point (.), a plus sign (+), and a minus sign (−).

Notice that most of the keys have an uppercase and a lowercase. For those keys, the numbers are the uppercase and other functions (explained later) are the lowercase. If you want to type the numbers, you must hold down the Shift key while you press the number keys.

The NumLock key works for the numeric keypad like the CapsLock key works for the alphabetic keys. If you press NumLock once, it locks the keypad in the numeric or uppercase. Press it again and the lowercase is restored.

(a) Suppose you want to type a 3 using the numeric keypad. What two keys would you press?____

(b) Suppose you want to enter several lines of numeric data using the numeric keypad. What key would you press first?________________________

Why?____

(c) What key would you press to restore the numeric keypad to its normal setting?____

— — — — — — — — — —

(a) Shift and 3; (b) NumLock, to lock the numeric keypad in the uppercase position; (c) NumLock again

6. When either the alphabetic keys or the numeric keypad is locked in uppercase (using CapsLock or NumLock), you can type a lowercase value for an affected key by holding down the Shift key. In other words, the Shift key *reverses* the setting for the key.

(a)   Suppose CapsLock is on and you want to type an "h". How would you do it?

____

(b)   Suppose NumLock is on and you want to use the Home function that shares

a key with "7". What keys would you press?_______________________

— — — — — — — — — —

(a) Shift and "h"; (b) Shift and "7"

7. At the left of the keyboard are the 10 program function keys, labeled F1 through F10. The 10 lowercase numeric keypad keys are also program function keys. Any program can use these 20 keys for whatever functions it likes. For example, we have a game program that uses the ←, →, ↑, and ↓ keys to position our spaceship and the F1 key to fire our rockets.

CP/M-86 uses these keys to save us from having to type frequently used commands. Thus, when you press F1, you see a directory of the disk in drive A, F2 displays a directory of the disk in drive B, and so forth. You will learn the standard CP/M-86 settings of each of the function keys as you study the CP/M-86 commands.

You can reset the meaning of any of the 20 function keys using the FUNCTION command, which you will study in Chapter Five.

(a)   How many program function keys are there?______________________

(b)   Ten of them are on the left side of the keyboard and are labeled F1 through

F10. Where are the others?

____

(c)   True or false? Every program can set its own functions for the program

function keys.____

(d) How does CP/M-86 use the program function keys?

    ____ A. As a shortcut for frequently used commands

    ____ B. To accomplish functions that cannot be accomplished with commands

(e) True or false? You cannot change the CP/M-86 settings for the function keys.

____

(a) 20; (b) the lowercase of the keys on the numeric keypad; (c) true; (d) A; (e) false—they can be changed with the FUNCTION command

THE CONTROL FUNCTIONS *Set 11.2 (11.4)*

8. As you type a command, it is stored in a special keyboard memory area. It is not sent to the CCP until you say so. You send a command to the CCP by pressing the Enter key.

As you type a command, you may make mistakes. Before you press Enter, you can correct those mistakes. The Backspace key is used to back up the cursor so you can overtype a character. The Backspace key erases as it backspaces.

(a) How do you send the line you have just typed to the CCP?___________

(b) How do you backspace and erase one character in the line you are typing?

____

(c) Match the key names with their symbols. (Not all the symbols are used; some aren't even real keys.)

    ____ A. Backspace   1. ↳

    ____ B. Enter   2. →

    3. ↵

    4. ⇤

    5. ←

(a) press Enter; (b) ← ; (c) A-5; B-3

9. Sometimes you need to type a command that is longer than the 80-character screen line. If you just keep typing, the cursor will automatically move to the beginning of the second line when it reaches the end of the first line. However, you can force the cursor to the beginning of the second line earlier than that if you wish. Just use Ctrl-E. That is, hold down the Ctrl (control) key and press the E key. The cursor will move to the beginning of the next line, but your command will not be sent to the CCP.

The Control key is not a character key. It is like a Shift key; when you hold it down, it changes the effect of some of the character keys that you type. You can use either uppercase or lowercase letters with Ctrl.

Match these keys with their descriptions.

_____ (a)   Enter

_____ (b)   Ctrl-E

_____ (c)   Ctrl

1.   Starts a new line but does not transmit command.
2.   Transmits command to CCP.
3.   No meaning; not used.
4.   Changes the meanings of character keys.
5.   Returns the cursor to the upper left corner.

— — — — — — — — — —

(a) 2; (b) 1; (c) 4

10. Sometimes you make so many mistakes typing a line that it's easier to start over than to correct it. You can eliminate the current line completely by pressing Ctrl-X. For example, suppose you have typed

    A>TXPT B;MUV_

If you press Ctrl-X, the line will look like this:

    A>_

Now you can start typing the command again.

Identify which keys you would press for the following functions.

(a)   Send the current line to the CCP. _________________________________

(b)   Eliminate the current line. ___________________________________

(c)   Erase the last character typed in the current line. ___________________

(d)   Start a new line without transmitting the command. ________________

— — — — — — — — — —

(a) Enter; (b) Ctrl-X; (c)   ; (d) Ctrl-E

11. There are two control functions that cause data to be sent to the printer (if you have one). The screen print function causes the current screen image to be printed. Screen print is the *uppercase* function of the key with this symbol: PrtSc. To select the screen print function, hold down the Shift key while you press the PrtSc key. Whatever shows on the console screen is printed on the printer.

You can also use echo printing. This means that each line that is displayed on the screen is simultaneously printed. Echo printing is activated by Ctrl-P. Hold down the Ctrl key and press the P key. This is a toggle function. If echo printing is off, it will be turned on. If it's on, it will turn off. (When you type a command, it is echo printed when you press Enter. When DOS displays a message, the message is echo printed as it is displayed.)

What is the difference between these two functions? Screen print causes 24 or fewer lines to be printed, whatever is currently on the screen. (What you see is what you get.) Echo printing causes all future data to be displayed, until you turn it off again. You might print 5 or 500 lines.

Suppose you want to print a copy of your disk directory. Would it be better to display it first and then print the screen or to turn on echo printing and then display the directory? Echo printing is probably better for this job because the directory might be longer than 24 lines.

(a) Match the two print functions with their descriptions.

_____ A. Screen print   1. Toggle function

_____ B. Echo print   2. Prints 24 lines or less
3. Copies lines until you turn it off again
4. Ctrl-P
5. ⇧-PrtSc

(b) Suppose echo printing is off. How do you turn it on?

____

(c) OK, now it's on. How do you turn it off again?

____

— — — — — — — — — —

(a) A-2, 5; B-1, 3, 4; (b) use Ctrl-P; (c) use Ctrl-P

Note: If you leave echo printing on while you run other CP/M-86 programs, it will slow those programs down because it takes longer to print data than to display it.

12.   Sometimes, after you enter a CP/M-86 command and it starts processing, you change your mind. You can terminate almost any program and return to the CCP using the break function, activated with Ctrl-C. Hold down the control key while you press the C key, and you will abruptly kill any CP/M-86 program that is running except the CCP itself. This symbol will be displayed: ^C. (All disks will also be given R/W status.)

Suppose you ask CP/M-86 to display a file and, as the data begins to roll onto the screen, you realize it's the wrong file. You don't have to wait until the whole file is displayed. You can cancel the command with Ctrl-C, then enter the correct command.

Sometimes, you just want to suspend a command without actually canceling it. For example, suppose you ask CP/M-86 to type a file that is longer than 24 lines. If you don't stop it, the beginning of the file will roll right off the top of the screen before you have a chance to read it (unless you're a very fast reader). Ctrl-S can be used to suspend a program. It just stops processing temporarily. When you press any character key, it will start again; a character key is a key that transmits a character to the system unit, such as x, the space bar or Enter.

So to view the entire file, let about 20 lines roll onto the screen, then press Ctrl-S. Read what's there, then restart the data again by pressing any character key. After another 15 or 20 lines have rolled past, suspend the program again. Continue scrolling and suspending until you have found what you're looking for or the file ends.

(a)   What do you press to suspend a program? __________________________

(b)   What do you press to cancel a program? __________________________

(c)   How can you resume a suspended program?

____

(d)   Which function causes a return to the CCP: the suspend function or the

break function?____

(e)   Suppose you enter a command to display the contents of a file, and it's going

past so fast you can't read it. What keys would you press?____________

(f)   Suppose after you start reading it, you find out it's the wrong file. What keys

would you press?____

__ __ __ __ __ __ __ __ __ __

(a) Ctrl-S; (b) Ctrl-C; (c) press any character key; (d) break; (e) Ctrl- S; (f) Ctrl-C

13. You have studied the control functions: enter, backspace, cancel a line, new line, break, suspend and resume, screen print, and echo print. These functions work when you are using CP/M-86 programs such as the CCP (and the built-in programs), as well as certain transient programs such as ED and PIP. They may or may not work with other transient programs, depending on how the programs are written. (You can kill *any* program by rebooting, Alt-Ctrl-Del.)

Which keys would you use for each function below?

(a) Transmit this line to the CCP:____

(b) Cancel this line:____

(c) Backspace:____

(d) Start a second line:____

(e) Suspend the program:____

(f) Kill the program:____

(g) Resume the program:____

(h) Print the screen (24 lines):____

(i) Echo print:____

(j) Stop echo printing:____

(k) Which of the following is true?

______ A. The control functions work with all programs on the Personal Computer.

______ B. The control functions work with CP/M-86 programs and some other programs.

______ C. The control functions work with CP/M-86 programs but not with any other programs.

— — — — — — — — — —

(a) Enter (↵); (b) Ctrl-X; (c) ← ; (d) Ctrl-E; (e) Ctrl-S; (f) Ctrl-C; (g) any character key; (h) Shift-PrtSc; (i) Ctrl-P; (j) Ctrl-P; (k) B

There are several more control keys you can use with CP/M-86 that duplicate functions you already know, or that are rarely, if ever, used. Briefly, they are:

see pg 11-4

> Ctrl-J:—same as Enter (↵).
> Ctrl-M:—same as Enter (↵).
> Ctrl-H:—same as Backspace (←).
> Ctrl-I:—same as Tab (→|).
> Ctrl-U:—discards current line (but doesn't erase it as Ctrl-X does).
> Ctrl-R:—redisplays current line.
> Ctrl-PrtSc:—same as Ctrl-P.
> Ctrl-Break:—similar to Ctrl-C but also turns off echo printing.
> Ctrl-NumLock:—same as Ctrl-S.
> Del:—similar to Backspace but displays erased character (very confusing).

GENERAL COMMAND FORMAT

Now that you know which keys to use to type your CP/M-86 commands, let's look at the format of a command.

14. To enter a CP/M-86 command you must be at command level. This means you must have a CP/M-86 prompt such as A>_ or B>_.

The general format of a CP/M-86 command is

> *d>programname operands*

The *d>* indicates the command prompt that's provided by the CCP. You don't type this. CP/M-86 displays the command prompt; when you type something, it will be put at the cursor position.

Programname is the name of the program you want CP/M-86 to execute. It must be either a built-in command or the name of a transient program on one of the drives.

If it's a transient program, it must be contained in a CMD file. CMD files are transient programs that have been translated into machine language and appropriately edited by the system so that they are completely ready to be run on your computer. Their file identifiers will always be in this format: *programname*.CMD. In the CP/M-86 command you enter only the programname; don't type the ".CMD".

The operands indicate what data the program should use. (An "operand" is something that is operated on.) In most CP/M-86 commands, the operands specify the names of files and disk drives. For example, in TYPE NEWDATA, the filename NEWDATA is the operand. Some CP/M-86 commands do not require operands.

The command is terminated by pressing Enter, which causes the CCP to process the command.

(a) Before you can type a CP/M-86 command, what must appear on your

terminal?____

(b) Programname must be the name of

_______ A. A CP/M-86 built-in command

_______ B. A CMD file on one of the drives

_______ C. Either of the above

_______ D. None of the above

(c) Suppose your A disk contains these files: TRUE.CMD, BLAST.CMD, and TEST.CMD. You want to run the TEST program, which doesn't use any operands. What entry do you make?

A>____

— — — — — — — — — —

(a) CP/M-86 prompt (such as A>); (b) C; (c) TEST

15. If a transient program is not stored as a file on the default drive, you must tell CP/M-86 where to find it. You can switch to the correct drive, as in

```
A>B:
B>CALC
```

You can also precede the programname with the drivename, as in

```
A>B:CALC
```

The major difference between these two techniques is the drive that remains active. In the first example, the B drive becomes the default drive; in the second example, the A drive remains the default drive.

For the following questions assume that your A disk contains TRUE.CMD, BLAST.CMD, and TEST.CMD and your B disk contains SORT.CMD, MERGE.CMD, and LIST.CMD.

(a) Show the entry or entries you would make if you want to run the SORT program but leave A the default drive.

A>____

(b) Show the entry or entries you would make if you want to run the LIST program and make B the default drive.

A>____

— — — — — — — — — —

(a) A>B:SORT
(b) A>B:
 B>LIST

16.   Here's the general command format again:

    d>programname operands

Some programs, as you've seen, do not involve operands. In these cases, you just type the programname and press the Enter key.

Many programs require a file identifier as an operand. If so, after the program-name, type at least one space and then the file identifier. If the file is on the default drive, you don't need to include the drivename. For example, if you want to erase the file named SOURCE.DAT from disk A, you could enter either of these commands:

    A>ERA SOURCE.DAT
    A>ERA A:SOURCE.DAT

If SOURCE.DAT is on disk B, you have three choices. You could switch the disks, but this isn't very practical. You could make B the default drive, or you could enter this command:

    A>ERA B:SOURCE.DAT

Most of the time when a command calls for a file identifier, you use both the filename and the filetype. We'll let you know when the filetype should be omitted.

(a)   Show the general format for a CP/M-86 command that does not require a file identifier.

    d>____

(b)   In a CP/M-86 command, *programname* is separated from *operands* by

____

(c)   In a file identifier, the drivename is:

______ A. Always needed

______ B. Sometimes needed

______ C. Never needed

(d)   When a file identifier is an operand, do you generally include the filetype?

____

(e)   You want to erase the INVENTY.EXE file on disk A. Show the fastest way to do this.

    B>ERA ____

(f)   You want to erase DATA3.DOC, which is on the disk in drive A. Code the command.

    A>____

(g)   You want to type the file named PROOF.DAT, which is on drive B. Code the command.

    A>TYPE ____

(h)   You want to use the program named COURSE, which is on drive B, and the file named STUDENTS.DAT, which is also on drive B. Code a command to do this *without* changing the default drive.

    A>____

(i)   Recode the above command so that drive B becomes the default drive.

    A>____

— — — — — — — — — —

(a) programname; (b) one or more spaces; (c) B; (d) yes; (e) B>ERA A:INVEN-TY.EXE (f) A>ERA DATA3.DOC or ERA A:DATA3.DOC (g) A>TYPE B:PROOF.DAT (h) A>B:COURSE B:STUDENTS.DAT [*Note:* If you didn't code the B: with STUDENTS.DAT, CP/M-86 would look for it on the *default* drive (A), even though you coded B: with the programname];
(i)   A>B:
    B>COURSE STUDENTS.DAT

17.   The built-in commands must not be preceded by drivenames, as they are not related to drives. (Recall that they are part of the CCP.)

(a)   Which of the following will type the file named INVENTY.DAT from drive B? (TYPE is a built-in command.)

    _____ A. A>TYPE B:INVENTY.DAT

    _____ B. A>B:TYPE INVENTY.DAT

    _____ C. A>B:
            B>TYPE INVENTY.DAT

(b) Which of the following may not be prefixed with drivenames?

    ____ A. Built-in commands

    ____ B. Transient commands

    ____ C. File identifiers

———————————

(a) A, C; (b) A

18. For the questions below, assume that you have two disks containing these files:

Drive A	*Drive B*
SORT.EXE	INVENTY.EXE
MERGE.EXE	INVENTY.DAT
SORT.DAT	PARTS.DAT

(a) Show the command(s) to run the SORT program using the file named PARTS.DAT as an operand. Leave drive A as the default drive.

A>____

____

(b) Show the command(s) to erase SORT.DAT. (ERA is a built-in command.) Leave drive B as the default drive.

B>____

____

(c) Show the command(s) to run the SORT program with the INVENTY.DAT as an operand. End up with drive A as the default drive.

B>____

____

———————————

(a) A>SORT B:PARTS.DAT
(b) B>ERA A:SORT.DAT
(c) B>A:
   A>SORT B:INVENTY.DAT

19. CP/M-86 can read uppercase or lowercase. It doesn't matter whether you type a command using all capital letters, all lowercase letters, or a combination of both. Our examples will always show input commands in all capital letters so you can differentiate them from CP/M-86 messages, which are in uppercase and lowercase.

Suppose you want to enter a command to erase the file named ACTION.COM. Which one of the following would be valid?

_____ (a)   A>ERA ACTION.COM

_____ (b)   A>Era ACTION.COM

_____ (c)   A>Era Action.Com

_____ (d)   A>era action.com

——————————————

all of them are valid

CP/M-86 COMMAND PROCESSING

20. Now that you have seen what a CP/M-86 command generally looks like, let's discuss what happens when you enter the command. First of all, CP/M-86 searches for the program you named as programname. If it's a built-in program, it's already a part of the CCP. It was loaded into memory when the system was booted. Otherwise CP/M-86 looks for the appropriate CMD file on the specified drive. (If no drive was specified, the default drive is assumed.)

If it can't find the correct program, the CCP returns an error message—the programname followed by a question mark. CP/M-86 does not search the other drive. Below is a sample printout in which we accidentally misspelled the ERA programname.

```
A>ERRA INVENTY.DAT
ERRA?

A>_
```

This message means the system can't recognize our programname. Either we misspelled it, or the appropriate CMD file is not on the specified drive.

The CP/M-86 prompt is then repeated, as shown in the above example, so that we can enter the correct command.

(a) When you enter a CP/M-86 command, what's the first thing the CCP does?

____

(b) Suppose you have the following interaction:

```
A>TYP JOHNSON.PRN
TYP?

A>_
```

What could be wrong?

_____ A. TYP is not a built-in command

_____ B. JOHNSON.PRN is not a file on the A disk.

_____ C. TYP is not a program on the A disk.

— — — — — — — — — —

(a) CP/M-86 searches for a file named programname.CMD or a built-in program; (b) A and C

21. If the CCP successfully locates your transient program on the specified disk, it reads the program from the disk into memory. You can hear this happening. If it's a short program, it could take less than a second to load. Longer programs may take 5 seconds or longer.

CP/M-86 also stores any operands in an area of memory where the transient program can find them. Control is then given to the beginning of the program. You are now out of command level and into program level.

What happens next depends entirely on the program. Most programs will check the filename(s) and other operands and display error messages if they aren't correct. You'll be learning more about this when you study the built-in and transient programs later on. If the operands are OK, the program may or may not display any messages. Many programs run perfectly without sending any messages to the user, as in this example:

```
A>SORT MERGDATA

     (5-second wait)

A>_
```

During the 5-second wait, the SORT program was located, loaded, and executed. It sorted the file named MERGDATA. Then it terminated, displaying no messages.

When the program terminates, the CCP resumes control, and you're back at command level again. You'll know when this occurs because you'll see the CP/M-86 command prompt. The terminated program is completely finished. There's no "residue" waiting to be reactivated. Your next command may refer to any program (even the same program all over again).

(a) Below is shown a typical CP/M-86 interaction.

```
A>MERGE B A

   (3-second wait)

A>_
```

Briefly describe what happened during the 3-second wait. (*Note:* MERGE is not a built-in command.)

____

____

____

____

Here's another interaction.

```
A>SORT INVENTY.DAT
FILE NOT FOUND_
```

(b) What program sent the error message?______________________________

(c) At what level are you now?______________________________

(d) Can you enter a CP/M-86 command now?______________________________

_ _ _ _ _ _ _ _ _ _ _

(a) CP/M-86 searched for and loaded the MERGE program, passed the operands to it, and gave it control; the MERGE program ran and terminated and CP/M-86 resumed control; (b) SORT; (c) program level; (d) no (you must have the CP/M-86 prompt to enter a CP/M-86 command)

Chapter Three Self-Test

You may refer to Figure 3.1 or the keyboard itself to answer questions 1 to 5.

1. Which key is next to the Ctrl key?
   a. A
   b. CapsLock
   c. Space bar
   d. ↵

2. Which key is next to the Enter key?
   a. Space bar
   b. Tab
   c. [4 ←]
   d. +

3. Which key is next to the NumLock key?
   a. Space bar
   b. Ctrl
   c. Shift
   d. ←

4. Which key is next to the PrtSc key?
   a. Shift
   b. Space bar
   c. Alt
   d. Esc

5. Which key is next to a Shift key?
   a. 0
   b. +
   c. NumLock
   d. \

6. Which key/s do you press for the following functions?

    a. Send a line to CCP: ____

    b. Screen print: ____

    c. Echo print: ____

    d. Suspend processing: ____

    e. Resume processing: ____

    f. Kill the program: ____

    g. Back up one character: ____

    h. Start a new line without sending the current one: ________________

    i. Shift the numeric keypad to uppercase: ____________________

    j. Shift the numeric keypad back to lowercase: ____________________

    k. Eliminate the current line and start over: ____________________

7. Suppose A is the default drive and you are using two disks:

    Drive A   *Drive B*

    LIST.CMD   PUSH.CMD
    SORT.CMD   PULL.CMD
    MOVE.CMD   INVENTRY
    LETTERA   ORDERS
    LETTERB   STOCK
    LETTERC

    a. Write a command to use the LIST program with the LETTERA file.

        A>____

    b. Write a command to use the SORT program and the STOCK file.

        A>____

    c. Write a command to use the PUSH program with the LETTERB file.
        Leave A the default drive.

        A>____

    d. Write a command to use the PULL program with the INVENTRY file.
        Leave A the default drive.

        A>____

    e. Write commands to use the PULL program with the STOCK file. Make
        B the default drive.

        ____

        ____

8. Suppose you have this interaction:

```
A>CRUSH LETTERD
CRUSH?

A>_
```

What is wrong?____

____

9. Can you use a drivename with a built-in command, as in A>B:TYPE

STOCK?____

10. Suppose you have this interaction:

```
A>SORT LETTERC

    (10-second pause)

A>_
```

Briefly describe what the computer did during the 10-second pause.

____

____

____

11. Which of the following should be used to type CP/M-86 commands?
    a. Uppercase letters
    b. Lowercase letters
    c. Either of the above

Self-Test Answer Key

1. a

2. c

3. d

4. a

5. d

6. a. Enter (↵) (or Ctrl-J or Ctrl-M)
   b. Shift-PrtSc
   c. Ctrl-P (or Ctrl-PrtSc)
   d. Ctrl-S (or Ctrl-NumLock)
   e. Any character key
   f. Ctrl-C (or Ctrl-Break or Ctrl-Alt-Del)
   g. Backspace (←) (or Ctrl-H)
   h. Ctrl-E
   i. NumLock
   j. NumLock
   k. Ctrl-X

7. a. A>LIST LETTERA
   b. A>SORT B:STOCK
   c. A>B:PUSH LETTERB
   d. A>B:PULL B:INVENTRY
   e. A>B:
       B>PULL STOCK

8. There is no CRUSH.CMD file on the A drive.

9. no

10. The SORT program was loaded and executed.

11. c

Suggested Machine Exercise

In this exercise, you'll practice typing and entering commands. You'll enter a lot of "bad" commands, just for practice. Don't worry about that. It doesn't hurt the computer in any way.

What You Should Do	*What the Computer Will Do*
1. Boot the system. (Refer to Chapter One machine exercise if you don't remember how to do this.)	Display the initial screen.
2. Try typing the following just to get used to the regular keyboard. Correct your mistakes with the backspace key. 1990 is the time for 46,235.78 good people to come to the aid of their parties. (See frames 1 to 4.)	Display each letter on the screen as you type it.
3. Press Enter (↵)	Try to process what you typed as a DOS command. Since it won't recognize the first word as a legitimate command, it will display this message: 1990?

4.   Retype the above in capital letters.
    a.   Press the CapsLock key once.
    b.   Type the above sentence so it looks like this:
 	
    1990 IS THE TIME FOR 46,235.78 GOOD PEOPLE TO COME TO THE AID OF THEIR PARTIES.
 	
(See frame 1.)
	Translate each letter to uppercase before displaying it.

5.   Eliminate what you have just typed.
    a.   Hold down the Ctrl key.
    b.   Press X.
(See frame 10.)
	Erase the sentence from its memory and from the screen.

6. Turn off CapsLock. a. Press the CapsLock key once. (See frame 1.)	Turn off the uppercase translation function.

7. Print a copy of your screen.
   a. Hold down the Shift (⇧) key.
   b. Press the PrtSc key.
 	
(See frame 11.)
	Copy each line from your CRT screen to the printer. Watch the cursor marking off each line as it is printed. Your printer may not print the status line exactly as it is on the screen.
	    If the screen did not print, you will need to locate and fix the problem before continuing. Make sure the printer is plugged in, turned on, loaded with paper, and hooked up to the system unit. If all that is true, get help from an expert.

8. Turn on echo printing.
   a. Hold down the Ctrl key.
   b. Press the letter P.
(See frame 11.)
	Turn on the echo printing function. (Nothing visible happens.)

9. Use the numeric keypad.
   a. Press NumLock once.
   b. Use the numeric keypad to type the following:
 	
    1230 + 456 − 789.5
 	
(See frame 5.)
	Nothing visible happens when you turn on the numeric keypad. The numbers are displayed as you type them. Echo printing does not work yet.

10. Press Enter.	The line you typed is echo printed. The computer tries to process the line as a CP/M-86 command and returns the message: 1230? This message is also echo printed.

11. The following instructions allow you to practice suspending and resuming.
   a. Type and enter this command: DIR
 	
   b. Hold down the control key and press the letter S.
   c. Press any character key. (Try the space bar.)
   d. Practice suspending and resuming the DIR program several times.
(See frame 12.)
	a. Begin displaying and echo printing a directory of the files on the disk in drive A.
	
	b. Suspend the output from the DIR program.
	c. Resume displaying and printing the directory.

12. Practice aborting a program.
    a. Type and enter DIR again.
 	
    b. Hold down Ctrl and press the letter C.
 	
(See frame 12.)
	a. Start displaying and printing the disk directory.
	b. Interrupt the directory, display ^C followed by the command prompt.

13. Continue practicing these functions until you're comfortable with them. Then shut down the system and go on to Chapter Four.	

CP/M-86 Built-In Commands

As you know, CP/M-86 has commands built into the console command processor (CCP). These built-in commands will display all or part of a disk directory, display file contents, erase files, change file identifiers, or change user numbers. In this chapter, you'll learn to use the CP/M-86 built-in commands to perform these functions.

When you complete your study of this chapter, you'll be able to:

- Code specific file-identifiers.
- Code generalized (wildcard) file references.
- Display or print all or part of a disk directory.
- Erase specified files from a disk.
- Change the name of a file on a disk.
- Display or print the contents of a (printable) file.
- Assign or change user number.

THE USER COMMAND

1.   When several people use the same computer and disks, they can each have different user numbers, from 0 through 15. This helps to keep one person from accessing another person's files.

Here's how the user numbers work: When you boot CP/M-86, the system assumes you are user 0. You enter a USER command to switch to your user number. Suppose you are user 3. You enter USER 3. The status line at the bottom will change to read U=03. Now if you create a new file, it will be stored on the disk for user 3 only. No other user can read, change, or erase this file; they can, however, copy it to their user number and read, change, or erase it there.

Obviously, user numbers do not provide much security. It's too easy to access other people's files by switching to their user numbers or by copying their files to your user number. The user numbers are meant to be a convenience. For example, when user 3 asks for a directory, only the files associated with user 3 are listed. Thus, user 3 doesn't have to wade through files belonging to other users. User numbers other than zero are frequently used with hard disks, which can hold hundreds of files. Keeping files under different user numbers helps to keep each person's directory down to a reasonable size.

(a) What is the lowest user number?_______________________________________

(b) What is the highest user number?______________________________________

(c) Code a command to switch from user 0 to user 6.

A>____

(d) Suppose you now create a new file. With what user number will it be associated?____

(e) Which of the following is true?

_____ A.   User 3 cannot write on user 6 files, but user 3 can read user 6 files.

_____ B.   User 3 can neither read nor write on user 6 files, but user 3 can copy user 6 files.

_____ C.   User 3 cannot access user 6 files in any way.

(f) True or false? If user 4 asks for a directory, only user 4 files will be listed.

____

(g) True or false? The user number system is meant to provide data security under CP/M-86.____

— — — — — — — — — —

(a) 0; (b) 15; (c) A>USER 6 (d) 6; (e) B; (f) true; (g) false—it's a convenience but not a security system

2. Files belonging to user 0 that have the SYS attribute are available to all user numbers. Remember that SYS files do not show up in a regular directory. SYS status is usually given to program files that are put on every disk. Suppose you want to put three CP/M-86 transient programs—PIP, ED, and STAT— on every disk and make them available to all users.

(a) What user number would you give them?____________________________

(b) What DIR/SYS status would you give them?__________________________

— — — — — — — — — —

(a) 0; (b) SYS

THE DIR COMMAND   *See   14.1 (14-1)*

3.   The DIR command is used to display the disk directory on the monitor. An entry like this:

```
A>DIR
```

results in a directory display for the current user number (nonsystem files only). If you want an echo print listing you can use Ctrl-P before entering DIR. The directory looks like this:

```
A>DIR
A: NEWFILE  BAK : NEWFILE         : ASM86  CMD : TOD      CMD
A: COPYDISK CMD : DDT86     CMD : ASSIGN CMD : NEWDISK CMD
A: FUNCTION BAK : PROTOCOL CMD : ED      CMD : SPEED    CMD
A: SUBMIT   CMD : HELP      CMD : HELP   CMD : STAT     CMD
A: GENCMD   CMD

SYSTEM FILE(S) EXIST
A>
```

The entries are formatted four across and separated by colons. Column 1 contains the drivename. The period that separates the filename from the filetype is not included. The message at the bottom tells you that this disk also contains some system files.

The directory listing of drive B can be obtained by entering a DIR B: command. (There must be a disk in drive B for the command to work.)

Suppose drive C is the default drive.

(a)   How can you display the regular directory for your user number?

   C>____

(b)   How can you display the regular directory for your user number on drive A?

   C>____

— — — — — — — — — —

(a) C>DIR (b) C>DIR A: (or C>A: followed by A>DIR)

4.   The DIR command can be used to list a single file if you include the filename as an operand. If you specify A>DIR GAME.ONE., you will get one of three responses. If drive A contains a nonsystem file named GAME.ONE for your user number, you'll get:

        A : GAME   ONE

If drive A doesn't contain that file, you'll get the message NO FILE. If drive A contains the file but it is a system file, you'll get the message SYSTEM FILE(S) EXIST.

  Figure 4.1 contains a list of files that might belong to one user number. For this list, which commands below would result in the message NO FILE?

_____ (a)   A>DIR COPY.CMD

_____ (b)   A>DIR TRY.NOW

_____ (c)   A>DIR FIVE

_____ (d)   A>DIR THREE.CH

— — — — — — — — — —

b; c (because there is no file with exactly that identifier, although there is a FIVE.CH)

(1) TRY	(10) PIP.CMD (system)	(19) CORRES.XX
(2) PRACTICE	(11) ED.CMD (system)	(20) CORRES.DK3
(3) THIS.NOW	(12) COPY.CMD (system)	(21) BILLING.DT
(4) ONE.CH	(13) INVOICE.XX	(22) SUPPLIES.DT
(5) TWO.CH	(14) INVOICE.WI	(23) PROGRAM.COB
(6) THREE.CH	(15) INVOICE.DK	(24) PROGRAM.REL
(7) FOUR.CH	(16) CORRES.WI	(25) PROGRAM.PRN
(8) FIVE.CH	(17) CORRES.DK1	(26) PROGRAM.DAT
(9) INTRO.CH	(18) CORRES.DK2	(27) PROGRAM.CMD (system)

Figure 4.1   File Listing, Drive A

5. Suppose you want to find out if your B disk contains the INVENTY.DAT file. Which of the following commands would limit the display to just that information?

_______ (a)   A>DIR B:

_______ (b)   A>DIR B:INVENTY.DAT

_______ (c)   A>DIR

_ _ _ _ _ _ _ _ _ _ _

b

Note: At this point you might want to stop studying for a few minutes and practice using the DIR command on your system.

6. The DIRS command differs from the DIR command in that it requests a directory of system files for the current user number. Here is an example:

```
A>DIRS
A: SPEED    CMD : SUBMIT   CMD : STAT     CMD
NON-SYSTEM FILE(S) EXIST
```

The message at the bottom tells you that this disk also contains some nonsystem files (files with directory status instead of system status).

If you enter DIRS followed by a file identifier, DIRS will look for just that system file for your user number. If there is none, you'll get the message NO FILE. If there is one, but it's a nonsystem file, you'll get the message NON-SYSTEM FILE(S) EXIST.

(a)   Code a command to list all the system files for your user number on drive B.

A>____

(b)   Code a command to list all the system files for your user number on the default drive.

A>____

(c)   Code a command to see if there is a system file named SORT.CMD for your user number on drive B.

A>____

(d)   Suppose the above command (question c) results in this message: NON-SYSTEM FILE(S) EXIST. What does this message mean?

_______ A.   There is no file named SORT.CMD, but the disk does contain some nonsystem files that should also be checked.

_______ B.   There is a nonsystem file named SORT.CMD on the disk.

—————————————

(a) A>DIRS B: (b) A>DIRS (c) A>DIRS B:SORT.CMD (d) B

7.   Suppose you are user 7, and your system has two disk drives. What commands would you use to find out all the files available to you? (Don't forget that user 0 system files are available to everybody.)

——————————————

here's one way to do it:

    DIR
    DIRS
    DIR B:
    DIRS B:
    USER 0 (to find out what system files are available under user 0)
    DIRS
    DIRS B:

THE ERA COMMAND *See 14.3 (14-4)*

8.   The ERA built-in command is used to erase files from the directory and from the disk. Here is its format:

    ERA file-identifier

The command ERA XYZ.PRN will erase the file of that name from the default disk, for the current user number. The space the file occupied is made available. The prompt is displayed after the file is erased. If a file of that name doesn't exist on the default drive for the current user number, the NO FILE message is displayed. Both DIR and SYS files can be erased by the ERA command.

(a)   Write a command to erase the first file from the list in Figure 4.1.

    A>____

(b)   Suppose you have the following dialogue with CP/M-86:

```
A>ERA B:FERNANDZ.LET
NO FILE
A>_
```

What happened?____

____

—————————

(a) A>ERA TRY; (b) there is no file of that name for the current user number on drive B, and so nothing was erased

9. Files associated with the current user number can be erased from any disk if you prefix the filename with the drivename. ERA B:XYZ.CMD will remove file XYZ.CMD from the disk on drive B and from the directory of drive B.
  Write commands to accomplish the following functions.

(a) Erase the file named INVENTY.DAT from disk A.

A>____

(b) Erase the file named COPY.CMD from disk C.

A>____

(c) Display the regular directory of disk C.

A>____

(d) Display the regular directory of disk A.

A>____

(e) Find out if COPY.CMD is on disk B for the current user number.

A>____

(f) Erase COPY.CMD from disk B.

A>____

(g) Check to see if COPY.CMD was erased from disk B.

A>____

—————————

(a) A>ERA INVENTY.DAT
(b) A>ERA C:COPY.CMD
(c) A>DIR C
(d) A>DIR
(e) A>DIR B:COPY.CMD (or DIR B: but DIR B:COPY.CMD is more efficient; you
    could use DIRS instead of DIR)
(f) A>ERA B:COPY.CMD
(g) A>DIR B:COPY.CMD

10.   Erasing a file involves writing on the disk directory. If a disk has been write protected, then you can't write on it, even to erase a file from it. If you try to erase a file from a write-protected disk, here's the message you'll get:

```
Disk A: Write protected R/I/C/D?
```

You have a choice of four options: R for retry, I for ignore, C to cancel the command, and D to request more details about the error. These four options are offered for every disk error message displayed on the status line. If you really want to erase this file from this disk, you can remove the disk, take off the write protect tape, put the disk back in, and type R for retry. You could also change to another disk before retrying the command. The I option doesn't make much sense as CP/M-86 will not ignore write protection. To cancel the ERA command, type C. You can ask for more details, using D, if you want, but CP/M-86 will not display any useful information in this situation. (There are other error messages where D does result in some useful information.) So your two main options here are to fix the disk and retry or to cancel the command.

If you try to write on a drive that is currently read-only (because you changed the disk and didn't type Ctrl-C), here's the message you'll get:

```
BDOS Err on B: R/O
```

This means that the BDOS program (remember that?) cannot write on an R/O drive. When you get this message, strike any key to clear the message. Then use Ctrl-C to make the disk R/W. Then you can reenter the command.

If you try to erase a file that has the read-only attribute, regardless of whether the drive has R/O or R/W status, here's the message you'll get: BDOS Err on B: File R/O. Strike any key to clear the error message. If you still want to erase the file, make it R/W (using STAT); then reenter the ERA command.

Suppose you have this interaction:

```
A>ERA FEBDATA
BDOS Err on A: File R/O_
```

(a)   Why can't you erase this file?______________________________________

(b)   How can you get back to command level?

____

(c)   How can you successfully erase this file?

____

Suppose you have this interaction:

```
A>ERA JUNEDATA
(beep!)
Disk A: Write protected R/I/C/D?
```

(d) Why can't you erase this file?_______________________________________

(e) How can you successfully erase this file?

____

(f) Instead, how can you kill the command and get back to command level?

____

Suppose you have this interaction:

```
A>ERA B:AUGDATA
BDOS Err on B: R/O_
```

(g) Why can't you erase this file?_______________________________

(h) How can you get back to command level?_______________________

(i) How can you successfully erase this file?_____________________

— — — — — — — — — —

(a) The file has read-only status; (b) type any character key; (c) change the file status to read/write, then reenter the ERA command; (d) the disk is write protected; (e) remove the write protection tab, then type R; (f) type C; (g) the drive is read-only; (h) type any character key; (i) type Ctrl-C then reenter the ERA command

THE REN COMMAND *See 14 (14-5)*

11.   The REN (rename) command is used to change the name of a file on a disk. REN just renames the file; it doesn't make another copy or move the file anywhere. REN is concerned only with the directory entry. Here is the format of the REN command:

REN new-file-identifier=old-file-identifier

Notice that the new file identifier is specified first, followed by an equal sign and the file identifier as it currently exists. You may use spaces around the equal sign if you wish. The command REN NEW.ONE=XYZ.PRN will change the identifier of the current file XYZ.PRN on the default drive to NEW.ONE.

Write commands to change file identifiers on the default drive as indicated below:

(a)   Change ONE.CH to CHAP1.BK

(b)   Change PROGRAM.CMD to PAYROLL.CMD

(c)   Change PRACTICE to TRYOUT.DOC

— — — — — — — — — —

(a) REN CHAP1.BK=ONE.CH
(b) REN PAYROLL.CMD=PROGRAM.CMD
(c) REN TRYOUT.DOC=PRACTICE

12.   Either or both of the file identifiers in the REN command can be preceded by a drivename. If you use a drivename on the second file identifier, it must match the drivename for the first file identifier. If not, CP/M-86 will question the second file identifier and won't rename anything. If you use a drivename on the first file identifier, only, the same drive will be assumed for the second file identifier. If a drivename is not included, the default drive will be used.

Indicate which drive will be used for each valid REN command below. If the command is invalid give the reason.

(a)   A>REN XYZ.PRN=XYZ.LST

(b)   A>REN A:XYZ.PRN=XYZ.LST

(c)   A>REN B:XYZ.PRN=A:XYZ.LST

(d)   A>REN XYZ.PRN=B:XYZ.LST

(e)   B>REN XYZ.PRN

(f)   A>REN B:XYZ.PRN=XYZ.LST

—————————

(a) drive A; (b) drive A; (c) invalid, drivenames are different; (d) invalid, drivenames are different; (e) invalid, only one file identifier is included; (f) drive B

13. Two more types of errors may arise when you issue REN commands. You may name an old file that doesn't exist or you may give a new name that already does exist. In either case, no file is renamed. Suppose your disk contains these files:

        FILE1.TEX   FILE1.BAK   TEX.COM
        FILE2.TEX   FILE2.BAK   PIP.COM
        FILE3.TEX   FILE3.BAK   ED.COM

You want to change FILE1.BAK to FILE1A.TEX. What happens if you code it like this?

        REN FILE1.BAK=FILE1A.TEX

First the system looks for the old file identifier in the directory, but FILE1A.TEX doesn't exist and you will get an error message "NO FILE". Suppose you reenter the line like this:

        REN FILE2.TEX=FILE1.BAK

Now the system can locate FILE1.BAK in the directory to change it. It also checks the directory to be sure it isn't duplicating a file identifier. In this case, FILE2.TEX is already in the directory and you get an error message "FILE EXISTS". If you really meant that last command, you would need to erase (ERA) or rename (REN) FILE2.TEX before renaming FILE1.BAK.

Refer once again to Figure 4.1. For each command below indicate the new file identifier or error message that results.

(a)   A>REN CORR.DK2=CORRES.DK2

____

(b)   A>REN A:TRY.OUT=TRY

____

(c)   A>REN THREE.CH=THREE.CHP

____

(d)   A>REN THREE.CH=PRACTICE

____

(e) A>REN A:FOUR.CHP=B:FOUR.CH

____

(f) A>REN PREFACE.CPM=INTRO.CH

____

— — — — — — — — — —

(a) new indentifier of CORRES.DK2 is CORR.DK2; (b) new identifier of TRY is TRY.OUT; (c) message NO FILE; (d) message FILE EXISTS; (e) error—different drivenames, message B:FOUR.CH?; (f) new identifier of INTRO.CH is PRE-FACE.CPM

14. The renaming operation requires writing on the disk and has the same restrictions that the erase operation has.

(a) Can you rename a file that is not under the current user number?________

(b) Can you rename a file on a R/O drive?________________________________

(c) Can you rename a file on a write-protected disk?____________________

(d) Can you rename a file that has R/O status?__________________________

(e) Can you rename a file that has SYS status?__________________________

— — — — — — — — — — —

(a) no; (b) no; (c) no; (d) no; (e) sure, why not?

15. Write commands to accomplish these operations on files from Figure 4.1.

(a) The INVOICE files are to be called BILL with the same filetypes.

____

____

____

(b) The PRACTICE file is to be named SIX.CH.

____

(c) BILLING.DT is to be changed to CORRES.WI. The old CORRES.WI can be removed.

____

____

————————————

(a) REN BILL.XX=INVOICE.XX, REN BILL.WI=INVOICE.WI, REN BILL.DK=INVOICE.DK; (b) REN SIX.CH=PRACTICE; (c) ERA CORRES.WI, REN CORRES.WI=BILLING.DT

THE TYPE COMMAND

16. The TYPE built-in command displays the contents of a file at the console. Here is the TYPE format:

> TYPE file-identifier

The file must contain printable characters such as textual material. Files of nonprintable characters such as CMD and some BAS files can be typed, but you'll see garbage (random characters and symbols) on the screen. (Your computer may also beep several times. This won't hurt the computer.)

(a) How can you use TYPE to produce a printed copy of a file on the printer?

(b) How can you temporarily stop a partially displayed file?_______________

(c) How can you restart it?____

(d) How can you permanently stop (abort) a file that is typing at the console?

____

————————————

(a) use Ctrl-P before carriage return; (b) use Ctrl-S; (c) type any character; (d) type Ctrl-C

17. Refer to Figure 4.1 again. Suppose A is the default drive and you enter this command:

> TYPE THIS.NEW

The system will respond with NO FILE—it couldn't find a file with that identifier. If you enter TYPETHIS.NOW, the system will respond TYPETHIS.NOW? because you left out the space and the CCP didn't recognize TYPE. If you enter TYPE THIS.NOW, the contents of that file will be displayed on the screen.

Write commands to display the contents of the files from Figure 4.1. Assume drive B is active.

(a) file (23)

> B>____

(b)   file (2)

   B>____

(c)   file (10)

   B>____

(d)   The CMD file isn't in printable form. How can you cancel the display?

   ____

— — — — — — — — — — —

(a) B>TYPE A:PROGRAM.COB
(b) B>TYPE A:PRACTICE
(c) B>TYPE A:PIP.CMD
(d) type Ctrl-C

18.   Refer to Figure 4.1 and write commands to perform the sequence of operations below.

(a)   Display a directory of all the nonsystem files for your user number.

   A>____

(b)   Remove the PROGRAM file with filetype PRN.

   A>____

(c)   Change the name of the PROGRAM.REL file to PATCH.REL.

   A>____

(d)   Display the contents of the PROGRAM file with filetype COB.

   A>____

(e)   Produce a printed listing of PROGRAM.COB.

   A>____

(f)   Stop the display of PROGRAM.COB in mid-TYPE.

   ____

— — — — — — — — — — —

(a) A>DIR
(b) A>ERA PROGRAM.PRN
(c) A>REN PATCH.REL=PROGRAM.REL
(d) A>TYPE PROGRAM.COB
(e) use Ctrl-P before the TYPE command is entered
(f) use Ctrl-S at the appropriate time

GENERALIZED FILE IDENTIFIERS   *See 11.5.4 (11-8)*

19.   A file identifier is used to locate a particular file or group of files on a disk. The file identifier is specific when it refers to a single file. Any file reference that includes the drivename, the filename, and the filetype refers to only one file and is specific. The drivename can be omitted if the appropriate disk is in the default drive.

A file identifier is generalized when it refers to a number of different files. One way of specifying a generalized file identifier is to use an asterisk (*) for either the filename or filetype, and the actual filename or filetype for the other. *.CMD refers to all the available files that have filetype "CMD," no matter what the specific filename is.

Label the file references below as specific or generalized.

(a)   B:INVENT.DEC ____

(b)   INVENT.* ____

(c)   A:*.DEC ____

(d)   INVENT.DEC ____

— — — — — — — — — — —

(a) specific; (b) generalized; (c) generalized; (d) specific

20.   A complete file identifier may include a drivename as well as a filename and filetype. Either the filename or the filetype, or both, can be replaced with an asterisk. The asterisk means that any combination of characters will do. The drivename cannot be replaced with an asterisk since a command can deal with only one disk drive at a time. However, the drivename can be omitted if the default drive is appropriate. Match the file identifiers with their descriptions.

_____(a)   A:*.PRN

_____(b)   B:JOBTIME.*

_____(c)   *:JOBTIME.PRN

_____(d)   *:*.*

_____(e)   A:*.*

_____(f)   B:*.CMD

1.   Invalid file identifier.
2.   Refers to all files on drive A with filetype PRN.
3.   Refers to all files on drive B with filename JOBTIME.
4.   Refers to all files on all disk drives.
5.   Refers to all files on the default drive.
6.   Refers to all files on drive B with filetype CMD.
7.   None of these.

— — — — — — — — — — —

(a) 2; (b) 3; (c) 1; (d) 1; (e) 5; (f) 6

21.   Suppose the default disk contains these files:

PAYROLL.COB   PIP.CMD
PAYROLL.REL   ED.CMD
PAYROLL.PRN   COPY.CMD
PAYROLL.DAT   DISKTST.CMD

Write file identifiers that refer to the files described below.

(a)   All the files that have PAYROLL as the basic filename.

____

(b)   All the files that have filetype CMD.

____

(c)   The COBOL source file (type COB) for the PAYROLL program.

____

(d)   All the files for this user number on this disk.

____

— — — — — — — — — —

(a) PAYROLL.*
(b) *.CMD
(c) PAYROLL.COB
(d) *.*

22.   You have seen how the asterisk is used to indicate a generalized filename or filetype. The asterisk indicates *any number* of characters—up to eight for the filename or three for the filetype.

You can also use a question mark (?) as a wildcard character. The reference ?TEST.DAT would be matched with any of these identifiers: ATEST.DAT, BTEST.DAT, CTEST.DAT, etc. But it would not be matched by NEWTEST.DAT or A1TEST.DAT. The ? can match only a single character in the corresponding position.

To answer the question below, assume that your default disk contains these files:

    PAYROLLS.COM
    PAYROLL1.DAT
    PAYROLL2.DAT
    PAYTAXES.COM
    PAYTAXES.DAT
    PAYROLLS.COB
    PAYTAXES.COB

(a) Name any files that match PAYROLL?.DAT.

____

(b) Name any files that match PAY?????.COM.

____

(c) Name any files that match PAYTAXES.CO?.

____

— — — — — — — — — —

(a) PAYROLL1.DAT and PAYROLL2.DAT
(b) PAYROLLS.COM and PAYTAXES.COM
(c) PAYTAXES.COM and PAYTAXES.COB

23.   The question mark can also be used in any position in a filename or filetype to refer to any character. The reference X?Z.* refers to any three-character filename that begins with X and ends with Z, no matter what the filetype is. These files would be included:

    XYZ
    XYZ.TEM
    X2Z.PRN
    XAZ.B

Suppose a disk contains these files:

    D330T1.WS
    D330B1.WS
    D330C1.WS
    D331T1.WST
    D331B1.WST
    D330C1.TWS

Write file identifiers to refer to the groups of files indicated below.

(a)   All the files whose filename ends with T1.

____

(b)   All the files whose filename includes 330.

____

(c)   All the files of filetype WS and filename ending with C1.

____

— — — — — — — — — —

(a) D33?T1.* or ????T1.*
(b) ?330??.*
(c) ????C1.WS

24.   Under CP/M-86 the filename always has eight characters while the filetype always has three characters. A blank is considered a specific character. The filename PIP.CMD is really PIPƀƀƀƀƀ.CMD, where ƀ indicates a blank. The filename TESTDATA is really TESTDATA.ƀƀƀ.

If you use the generalized identifier P?.CMD, you have really specified P?ƀƀƀƀƀƀ.CMD. To match this particular identifier, a file identifier will have blanks in positions 3 through 8; that is, it must be no more than two characters long. These identifiers would match: P1.CMD, PT.CMD, and P.CMD. But the identifiers PIP.CMD and PAYROLLS.CMD would not match.

Suppose a disk contains these files:

XYZ.A	XYZ	X006.A
XYY.A	XYX	X007.A
XYY.B	WALL	X008.B
XYX.B	ROOM	X009.C

Which files are included by each file identifier below?

(a)   ???.*______________________________________

(b)   ??X.*______________________________________

(c)   *____

(d)   X???????.A________________________________

(e)   X???.B____________________________________

(f)   X??.B_____________________________________

— — — — — — — — — —

(a) XYZ.A, XYY.A, XYY.B, XYX.B, XYZ, XYX; (b) XYX.B, XYX; (c) XYZ, XYX, WALL, ROOM: (d) XYZ.A, XYY.A, X006.A, X007.A; (e) XYY.B, XYX.B, X008.B; (f) XYY.B, XYX.B

25. In writing generalized file identifiers the asterisk is really an abbreviation that fills the rest of a filename or filetype with question marks. Look at these examples:

TE*.PRN	is equivalent to TE??????.PRN
TE*.*	is equivalent to TE??????.???

Characters following an asterisk are ignored by CP/M-86. Thus, *EE.COM is equivalent to *.CMD or ????????.CMD. The asterisk causes the name it appears in to be followed with question marks. This will create the generalized file identifiers.

The files in Figure 4.1 are numbered for your convenience. Indicate which files match each file identifier below.

(a) * ____

(b) T??.* ____

(c) T*.CH ____

(d) C*.* ____

(e) C*.D* ____

(f) *.WI ____

(g) *ES.D* ____

(h) P*.C* ____

(i) P* ____

— — — — — — — — — —

(a) 1, 2; (b) 1, 5; (c) 5, 6; (d) 12, 16, 17, 18, 19, 20; (e) 17, 18, 20; (f) 14, 16; (g) 15, 17, 18, 20, 21, 22, 26 (don't forget that the characters following * will be ignored); (h) 10, 23, 27; (i) 2

Now that you've learned how to write a generalized file identifier, let's practice some DIR and ERA commands. TYPE and REN require specific filenames since only one file can be typed or renamed at a time.

26.   In the DIR command the file identifier can be specific or generalized, as in these examples:

B:	This requests a directory of all files for the current user number on drive B.
.	This refers to all files for the current user number on the default drive.
X??.*	This is a typical generalized file identifier.
XYZ.CMD	This refers to a specific file.

Write two different commands to display the complete regular directory for the current user number on the default drive.

(a) ____

(b) ____

What is the general effect of each DIR command below?

(c) DIR *____

____

(d) DIR *.*____

____

(e) DIR *.CMD ____

____

(f) DIR T*.PRN ____

____

(g) DIR T?6?.PRN _______________________________________

____

— — — — — — — — — —

(a) DIR; (b) DIR *.*; (c) list all files with no (or blank) filetype; (d) list entire directory; (e) list all CMD files (filetype CMD); (f) list all PRN files with filename beginning with T; (g) list all PRN files that have filenames of three or four characters with T in the first position and 6 in the third

27. Refer to Figure 4.1. Assume drive A is active. Which of the DIR commands below will return the NO FILE message?

_____ (a)   DIR CORRE.*

_____ (b)   DIR PRACTICE.*

_____ (c)   DIR PROGRAM

_____ (d)   DIR *.CH?

_____ (e)   DIR IN??.*

_____ (f)   DIR IN*.*

_____ (g)   DIR XYZ.CMD

– – – – – – – – – – – –

(a) no filename is CORRE.; (c) no PROGRAM filename has a blank filetype; (e) no filename starting with IN has only four characters; (g) no file with that name is on the disk

28. Use Figure 4.1 and give the numbers of file identifiers that would be included in directory listings produced by these DIR commands.

(a)   DIR PRACTICE.*____

(b)   DIR *.CH?____

(c)   DIR IN*.*____

(d)   DIR CO???.*____

(e)   DIR P*.*____

(f)   DIR ??V*.*____

– – – – – – – – – – – –

(a) 2; (b) 4, 5, 6, 7, 8, 9; (c) 9, 13, 14, 15; (d) 12; (e) 2, 10, 23, 24, 25, 26, 27; (f) 8, 13, 14, 15

29. The ERA command can also reference a generalized file identifier. Refer again to Figure 4.1 Which files will be removed from the disk by each ERA command below?

(a)   ERA PRACTICE____

(b)   ERA PROGRAM.*____

(c)   ERA CORRES.DK2____

(d)   ERA *.CMD____

(e) ERA F*.CH____

(f) ERA T??.CH____

(g) ERA XYZ.CMD____

(h) ERA BILLING.DT____

(i) ERA *____

— — — — — — — — — —

(a) 2; (b) 23–27; (c) 1; (d) 10–12, 27; (e) 7, 8; (f) 5; (g) none; (h) 21; (i) 1, 2

30.   All files can be erased for a user number with the command ERA *.*. When you enter this command, CP/M-86 asks you to confirm the command by displaying the message "ALL (Y/N)?". If you enter "Y," all files for that user number are erased. If you enter "N," the ERA *.* command is canceled and nothing is erased.
   Suppose you have disks on drives A and B that contain these files:

Drive A	Drive B
PROGRAM.COB	TRY
PROGRAM.REL	PRACTICE
PROGRAM.PRN	THIS.NOW
PROGRAM.DAT	INVOICE.XX
PROGRAM.CMD	INVOICE.DK
PIP.CMD	INVOICE.WI
ED.CMD	

   Write commands to accomplish the following functions, working from the default drive indicated.

(a) Remove PIP.CMD from disk A.

   A>____

(b) Display the complete directory of the disk on drive B.

   A>____

(c) Remove files TRY and PRACTICE from drive B.

   A>____

(d) Change the default drive to B.

   A>____

(e) Remove all the PROGRAM files from drive A.

   B>____

(f) Remove the INVOICE files from drive B.

B>____

(g) Display the directory listing for drive A.

B>____

(h) Sketch the resulting display.

____

____

____

— — — — — — — — — —

(a) A>ERA PIP.CMD
(b) A>DIR B:
(c) A>ERA B:*
(d) A>B:
(e) B>ERA A:PROGRAM.*
(f) B>ERA INVOICE.*
(g) B>DIR A:
(h) A:ED   CMD

31.   Refer to Figure 4.1. Write commands to erase files as indicated below.

(a) Remove files (4) through (9).

A>____

(b) Remove all the files.

A>____

(c) Remove files (16) through (20).

A>____

— — — — — — — — — —

(a) ERA *.CH
(b) ERA *.*
(c) the shortest answer is ERA COR*.*

32. You can see that generalized file identifiers are handy for accessing groups of files. Keep that in mind when you are creating your file identifiers. Try to give files you might want to access as a group, identifiers that are similar to each other and different from your other files. Establishing a prefix system helps. For example, you might use the prefix INV on all your inventory files. Your inventory master file could be called INVMAST; your update program could be called INVUPDAT.CMD, your search program could be called INVSERCH.CMD, your backorder data could be called INVBACKO, and so forth. If you also have files of your inventions, be sure not to use the INV prefix for them. (You could use VEN.)

Now suppose you want a directory of all your inventory files. You can enter A>DIR INV*.*. If you want to erase them, you could enter A>ERA INV*.*.

Suppose you are creating a set of files containing the four chapters of your term paper for your American History class.

(a) What would you name the file containing Chapter 1?______________

(b) What would you name the file containing Chapter 2?______________

(c) What would you name the file containing Chapter 3?______________

(d) What would you name the file containing Chapter 4?______________

(e) How would you get a directory of all four files? A>______________

(f) How would you erase all four files? A>______________

— — — — — — — — — —

(a) we would call it HISTERM1; (b) we would call it HISTERM2; (c) we would call it HISTERM3; (d) we would call it HISTERM4; (e) we would enter A>DIR HISTERM*; (f) we would enter A>ERA HISTERM*

(1)	PIP.CMD	(8)	SUPPLY.FIL	(15)	SALES.DOC
(2)	ED.CMD	(9)	COPY.DOC	(16)	SALES.HST
(3)	COPY.CMD	(10)	SUPPLY.DOC	(17)	SALES.FIL
(4)	SUPPLY.ASM	(11)	RECORDS.LOC	(18)	ST.LST
(5)	SUPPLY.REL	(12)	RECORDS.STT	(19)	ST.DOC
(6)	SUPPLY.PRN	(13)	RECORD.ORD	(20)	DISK.DOC
(7)	SUPPLY.CMD	(14)	RECL.AV		

Figure 4.2 Files on Drive B for User 3

Chapter Four Self-Test

This Self-Test will help you determine if you have mastered the objectives of this chapter. Answer each question to the best of your ability. Then check your answers in the answer key at the end of the test.

These questions are based on the disk containing the files shown in Figure 4.2.

1. Write a command to switch to user 3.

   A>____

2. Write a command to display the directory of nonsystem files for the current user number.

   A>____

3. Write a command to display all directory entries with filenames beginning with S, no matter what the filetype is. (Notice that we switched to drive B.)

   B>____

4. Write a command to remove all files with filetype DOC from drive B.

   B>____

5. Write a command to change the name of RECL.AV to REC.ASM.

   B>____

6. Write a command to display the contents of file SUPPLY.FIL on the console.

   B>____

7. Suppose SUPPLY.FIL contains about 200 lines of data. How can you read the first few lines at your console?

   ____

8. How can you produce a printed copy of SUPPLY.FIL on the line printer?

   ____

9. Write a command to display a directory of all system files for your user number that have filetype CMD.

   B>____

10. Consider the files shown in Figure 4.2. Suppose you have just booted. You have several things to do.

   - Switch to user 3.
   - Erase files (11), (12), and (13).
   - Type printed copies of files (15) and (17).
   - Change the name of file (18) to STATES.
   - Change the name of SUPPLY.FIL to be INVENTY.DAT.
   - Examine the complete directory listing for your user number at the console.

   Write all the commands you would need. Show the prompt at the beginning of each line to indicate the default drive.

Self-Test Answer Key

Compare your answers to the Self-Test with the correct answers given below. If all your answers are correct you are ready to go on to the next chapter. If you missed any questions, you may find it helpful to review the appropriate frames from this chapter.

1. A>USER 3

2. A>DIR B: or DIR B:*.*. Alternatively, you could switch drives then issue DIR.

3. B>DIR S*.*, DIR S?????.*, DIR S??????.*, or DIR S???????.*

4. B>ERA *.DOC or ERA ????????.DOC

5. B>REN REC.ASM=RECL.AV

6. B>TYPE SUPPLY.FIL

7. Type Ctrl-S as soon as several lines appear on the console.

8. Type Ctrl-P before entering the TYPE command.

9. B>DIRS *.CMD

10. A>USER 3

A>B:	If you omitted this step, your file references all need the drive prefix)
B>ERA RECO*.*	(R*.* or REC*.* will also erase file (14))
B>TYPE SALES.DOC	(Enter Ctrl-P first)
B>TYPE SALES.FIL	(Enter Ctrl-P after)
B>REN STATES=ST.LST	
B>REN INVENTY.DAT=SUPPLY.FIL	
B>DIR	(or DIR *.*)

Suggested Machine Exercise

Now that you've used the machine a few times, you don't need quite as much help in the suggested machine exercise. From now on, we'll just list the steps you should follow.

1. Boot the system.
2. Install another disk in drive B. (Don't forget Ctrl-C.)
3. Get a directory of A disk.
4. Get a directory of B disk.
5. If you have a line printer, turn on echo printing and get a directory of disk A. Notice how much slower the output is. Turn off echo printing.
6. Get another directory of A, and this time interrupt the display and start again.
7. Rename PIP.CMD as COPY.CMD. (If your disk already has COPY.CMD, rename PIP.CMD as PIP2.CMD.)
8. Check the directory for all CMD files. PIP.CMD should not appear but your new name should.
9. Change the file with a new name—PIP2.CMD or COPY.CMD—back to PIP.CMD again and recheck the directory.
10. Change to user 2.
11. Check your directory. Are there any files for user 2?
12. Go back to user 0 and check the directory.
13. Try to type PRACTICE.PRN. You should get an error message.
14. Try to erase PRACTICE.PRN. Do you get a message?
15. Try getting some directories using generalized file references.
    a. Get a directory of all files with filetype CMD.
    b. Get a directory of all files with filetype BAS.
    c. Get a directory of all files whose filenames start with S.

This completes the suggested machine exercise for Chapter Four. Shut down your system and go on to Chapter Five.

CP/M-86 Transient Programs

The commands you learned to use in the last chapter are built into the console command processor of CP/M-86. Your system disk also contains various transient programs that are supplied as part of CP/M-86. These transient programs can be used to get information about your disks, perform common operations, create files, and assemble or compile new programs.

In this chapter we overview the transient programs routinely supplied as part of the CP/M-86 system disk. You will also learn how to use several of them. You probably won't use all of the CP/M-86 transient programs, but it's a good idea to know what is available. As you use CP/M-86 on the job, you'll quickly learn which of these transient programs you'll need to use a great deal.

When you complete this chapter, you will be able to:

- Differentiate between built-in and transient programs.
- Identify the CP/M-86 transient programs that would be used to perform various functions.
- Use the HELP command to look up information about other commands.
- Use the NEWDISK command to format a new disk.
- Use the COPYDISK command to copy a disk.
- Use the FUNCTION command to change the meaning of a function key.
- Use the TOD command to set the date and time.

TRANSIENT VERSUS BUILT-IN PROGRAMS

1. In the last chapter you learned to use the CP/M-86 built-in commands. These are built into the CP/M-86 system and are included in the system tracks on a disk. Whenever CP/M-86 is running, those built-in commands are present and can be used.

Now we're going to look at the transient programs. These are programs provided in addition to the CP/M-86 system itself. They aren't included on the system tracks; so a disk that contains the CP/M-86 system might not necessarily include all of these. However, your master disk will have them. You'll want to copy the transient programs you use regularly onto many of your disks.

(a) How are built-in programs different from transient programs, in terms of where they are located on a disk?

____

____

(b) Which type of CP/M-86 programs are automatically included on any disk that contains the CP/M-86 system?

____

____

(c) What type of CP/M-86 program might *not* be included on every disk that contains the CP/M-86 system?

____

— — — — — — — — — — — —

(a) built-in programs are on system tracks, and transient programs are on other tracks; (b) built-in; (c) transient

2.   The transient programs provided with CP/M-86 serve several purposes. We'll overview all of them in this chapter. Later chapters are devoted to a more detailed study of some of the major CP/M-86 transients.

Each CP/M-86 transient program is on the disk in the form of a file of filetype CMD [also called a CMD (command) file]. They are run by entering the filename (without CMD) and any required parameters. As you learn to use each program, you'll see what parameters are required for each. Here is a dictionary listing of a CP/M-86 disk that contains the standard CP/M-86 transient programs:

```
A : ASM86      CMD : TOD        CMD : COPYDISK CMD : DDT86      CMD
A : ASSIGN     CMD : NEWDISK    CMD : FUNCTION CMD : PROTOCOL CMD
A : ED         CMD : SPEED      CMD : PIP       CMD : SUBMIT    CMD
A : HELP       CMD : HELP       HLP : STAT      CMD : GENCMD    CMD
```

Which of the programs below can be run from this disk:

_______ (a)   TYPE

_______ (b)   SUBGEN

_______ (c)   PIP

_______ (d)   REN

_______ (e)   TOD

_______ (f)   ED

————————————

a, c, d, e, f (a and d are built-in and available on every system disk; SUBGEN, choice b, is not on the disk)

THE ED PROGRAM

3.   The ED program is CP/M-86's text editor. You use it to make new files or change old ones. ED is concerned with "ASCII" (text) files, which are made up of strings of characters. Typical ASCII files might be correspondence, a chapter in a book, a mailing list, or a source program written in any language supported by the computer. A CMD file is not an ASCII file. ("ASCII" stands for "American Standard Code for Information Interchange.")
   To use ED, you enter a command in this format:

> ED specific-file-identifier

If the file you specify exists, ED will let you change it or add to it. If the file doesn't exist, ED will create a directory entry and let you put information in the file. You can determine what filetype to use by the kind of data the file can provide. For example, an assembly language source program file should have type A86. Other programs require such types as COB (COBOL), FOR (Fortran), or PLM (PL/M). Most other files may have whatever filetype seems appropriate. Many files have no filetype at all. We'll cover ED in detail later in this book.
   Suppose a disk contains only these files: ED.CMD, PROG1.A86, and PROG1.TEX.

(a)   What can you do with PROG1.TEX after you enter the command shown

below? ____

> AED >PROG1.TEX

(b)   What command will let you create a file called TWO.DAT?

A>____

(c)   What command will let you modify the assembly language source program?

A>____

————————————

(a) change it or add to it
(b) A>ED TWO.DAT
(c) A>ED PROG1.A86

THE PIP PROGRAM

4. The PIP program (PIP.CMD) is CP/M-86's file-handling utility program. With PIP (it stands for Peripheral Interchange Program) you can copy files from one disk to another or from a disk to any peripheral device. In fact PIP does all the internal conversions needed to load, print, punch, copy, and combine disk files. What you can do with PIP is limited only by the peripheral devices of your system. Chapter Seven is devoted entirely to PIP.

PIP is used to transfer files from a disk to any output device. When you want a transient program to be copied to a new disk, you need to PIP it over. Any file, of any filetype, can be PIPped.

PIP can also be used to make another copy of a file on the same disk—under a different name or a different user number.

(a) Which of these can be copied to another disk with PIP?

    _____ A. ED.CMD

    _____ B. ERA

(b) Which of these transfers can be performed using PIP?

    _____ A. Disk to disk

    _____ B. Printer to disk

    _____ C. Disk to printer

____

(a) A; (b) A and C

STAT AND SUBMIT

5. The STAT transient program provides general status information about a disk, a user number, or a file. STAT tells you the size of a file and its attributes. It tells how much space is left on a disk or how many (and which) user numbers have files on the disk. You can also use STAT to change the file attributes. You'll learn to do this in the next chapter.

The SUBMIT transient program lets you use a single command to execute a series of CP/M-86 commands. To use SUBMIT, you must first create a file of type SUB. This SUB file contains other CP/M-86 commands and parameters. When you execute the SUB file, each command is executed in turn. In the final chapter of this book, you'll learn to create your own files for submitting to CP/M-86.

(a)   What program provides status information about files or disks?

____

(b)   What program lets you execute a series CP/M-86 commands by entering a
single command?____

(c)   What program is used to create a new file?_____________________________

— — — — — — — — — — —

(a) STAT; (b) SUBMIT; (c) ED

6.   Identify the CP/M-86 transient program that would be used to accomplish
each function below:

(a)   Copy a file from one disk to another. ______________________________

(b)   Copy a file from one disk to another, erase the original file, and list the
directory of the source disk—with a single command. ______________

(c)   Identify the user numbers in use on a particular disk. ________________

(d)   Modify the contents of an ASCII file. ______________________________

— — — — — — — — — —

(a) PIP; (b) SUBMIT; (c) STAT; (d) ED

PROGRAM-RELATED TRANSIENTS

Three of the CP/M-86 transient programs are closely related to programming
your microcomputer. This book will not teach you how to write Assembly
Language programs. However, it will show you how to code the ASM86,
GENCMD, and DDT86 commands to invoke these transient programs. You'll
also learn what is needed as input and produced as output for each of the
programs.

7.   The ASM86 program is the CP/M-86 assembler. It translates a source file
written in 8086 or 8088 Assembly Language into your machine's internal language—the only language that your computer can understand.
   If you are going to program your computer using assembly language, this is
what you would do. Use ED to create a source file of Assembly Language
commands. The filetype must be A86; for example, you might create a file named
PAY7.A86.

Then use the ASM86 program to *translate* the file into machine language. ASM86 takes a file with filetype A86, "assembles" it, and produces three output files. All output files have the same filename as the A86 file, but one has filetype LST, the second has filetype H86, and the third has filetype SYM.

The LST file is meant to be displayed or printed. It contains a listing of the translated program and any messages from ASM86 to the programmer. The H86 file contains the translated program. The SYM file is a cross-reference listing between the source program and the H86 program, including the symbolic names.

Suppose your disk contains these files: ASM86.CMD, GENCMD.CMD, PAY7.A86, MAIL.A86 and MAIL.DAT. A command like this will assemble the PAY7 program:

    A>ASM86 PAY7

The filetype isn't entered, although it must be A86. This command invokes the CP/M-86 assembler and produces as output PAY7.LST, PAY7.H86, and PAY7.SYM.

(a) Write a command to assemble the MAIL.A86 file.

    A>____

(b) What readable file is produced as output?

    ____

(c) What other files are produced as output?

    ____

———————————————

(a) ASM86 MAIL; (b) MAIL.LST; (c) MAIL.H86 and MAIL.SYM

8. The GENCMD program is used to convert an H86 file to a CMD file. This turns the file into a command file that is executable as a transient program by typing the filename and pressing Enter. If you enter the command

    A>GENCMD PAY7

the file PAY7.H86, created by ASM86 PAY7, is "loaded" and translated into machine executable code. The output is then filed on disk as PAY7.CMD. You can now enter the command PAY7 and run the program.

As you can see, once you can write programs in 8086 or 8088 Assembly Language, this method will enable you to create new transient programs that run under CP/M-86.

(a) What filetype is needed for input to GENCMD?_______________________

(b)   Write a command to load the file produced by the command ASM86 MAIL.

A>____

(c)   What file will contain the output? ____________________________

— — — — — — — — — —

(a) H86; (b) A>GENCMD MAIL (c) MAIL.CMD

9.   Most Assembly Language programs (in fact, most programs) don't work perfectly the first time. They need to be tested and debugged. (Debug is a quasi-technical term for "getting the bugs out," or making a program work correctly.) CP/M-86 provides the DDT86 transient program as a dynamic debugging tool to help programmers debug their Assembly Language programs, after being assembled as CMD files. We're not going to go into details of DDT86 here, but programmers can interact with the computer as they test and run their programs.

(a)   What is the DDT86 program used for?______________________________

____

(b)   What type of file can be tested with the DDT86 program?

____

— — — — — — — — — — —

(a) debugging Assembly Language programs: (b) CMD

10.   Name the CP/M-86 program (built-in or transient) that can accomplish each function below.

(a)   Copy program files to a different disk.________________________

(b)   Change the name of a file.________________________________

(c)   Convert an H86 file to a CMD file.____________________________

(d)   Debug a CMD file.______________________________________

(e)   Create an ASCII (printable) file from the keyboard.________________

(f)   Translate A86 file to a H86 file.______________________________

(g)   Determine the amount of space left on a disk.__________________

— — — — — — — — — — —

(a) PIP; (b) REN; (c) GENCMD; (d) DDT86; (e) ED; (f) ASM86; (g) STAT

HARDWARE ASSIGNMENTS

11. Three commands are used to change hardware assignments in your system: ASSIGN, PROTOCOL, and SPEED.

ASSIGN is used to change the assignment of a physical device (a piece of equipment) to a logical device (a CP/M-86 I/O function). CP/M-86 has four logical devices that it uses in its programs. CON: is the console (the device that inputs commands and displays messages); it is usually assigned to the SCREEN and the KEYBOARD physical devices. LST: is the listing device that receives CP/M-86 print data as a result of echo printing, screen printing, etc.; it is usually assigned to the physical device named PRINTER-0. The other two logical devices, AXI: and AXO:, are auxiliary devices and are not normally assigned to hardware devices. If you want to change the assignment of any of these devices, you use the ASSIGN command. For example, suppose you have a letter quality printer hooked up to serial port 0 and you want to use it as the listing device. You would enter A>ASSIGN LST: SERIAL-0.

PROTOCOL is used specifically for a device connected to a serial port. Such devices frequently use same kind of method to let the computer know when they are and are not ready to receive data. These communication methods are known as protocols; the two commonly used protocols are XON and ETX. If you hook a device up to a serial port, you'll need to use the PROTOCOL command to tell CP/M-86 whether that device uses XON, ETX, or no (NONE) protocol.

You will also need to tell CP/M-86 the transmission speed and other communication characteristics of the serial device. The SPEED command is used to do this.

Obviously, we haven't told you enough about these commands to enable you to use them. If you install any extra boards and devices in your system, you'll need to use your CP/M-86 manual as well as the device manuals to get CP/M-86 to communicate with the new device(s) properly.

To answer the following questions, write the name of the commands. Don't try to code the actual commands.

(a) What command lets you change the assignment of a physical device to a logical device?____

(b) Suppose you want to use the device hooked up to the printer-l port as the output console device. What command would you use to make the change?

____

(c) Suppose you hook up a telephone communication with another computer to serial port 1. What command would you use to tell CP/M-86 to send data at 960 characters per second to that port?

____

(d) What command would you use to tell CP/M-86 to use the ETX protocol with that serial port?____

————————————

(a) ASSIGN; (b) ASSIGN; (c) SPEED; (d) PROTOCOL

THE HELP PROGRAM

12. The HELP program gives you some assistance at your computer with commands; so you don't have to go back to your manuals to look up command details.

To use HELP, you can just enter the command HELP. You will see a display like this:

```
HELP UTILITY Vn.n

At "HELP>" enter topic  {,subtopic}. . .

EXAMPLE: HELP> DIR EXAMPLES

Topics available:

ASM86          ASSIGN        COMMANDS
COPYDISK       DDT86         DIR
DIRS           ED            ERA
FUNCTION       FILENAME      GENCMD
HELP           NEWDISK       PIP
PROTOCOL       REN           SPEED
STAT           SUBMIT        TOD
TYPE           USER

HELP>
```

This is the main HELP menu and it tells you what topics are available. (You may have a different version than we do, so your menu might be a little different.)

Let's look at the TYPE topic. We would enter this:

```
HELP>TYPE
```

The response is

```
TYPE

FORMAT: TYPE filespec

PURPOSE:

    Displays contents of an ASCII
file on the screen. Press any key
to discontinue the display.  TYPE
does not accept wildcard filespecs.
Entering a ^P prior to the type
command causes the output to be
echoed to the printer until another
^P is entered.

Additional topics available:

EXAMPLES

HELP>
```

This display tells you the main points about the TYPE command. It also tells you that you can request some examples of TYPE. To see those examples, you must enter HELP>TYPE EXAMPLES. If you just entered HELP>EXAMPLES, the HELP program would not know which examples you wanted to see. (Most of the topics have an EXAMPLES subtopic.)

To end the HELP program and get back to the CCP, just press Enter in response to the HELP> prompt.

(a) Write a command to start the HELP program and display the HELP main menu.

A>____

(b) Write a command to view the topic that explains filenames.

HELP>____

(c) Write a command to view the EXAMPLES subtopic of the DIR topic.

HELP>____

(d) How do you terminate the HELP program?_________________________

— — — — — — — — — —

(a) A>HELP
(b) HELP>FILENAME
(c) HELP>DIR EXAMPLES
(d) just press Enter when HELP> displays

13.   You can bypass the main HELP menu and go straight to the topic or subtopic of your choice by entering a command in this format:

> A>HELP topic subtopic

For example, to see some examples for the DIRS command, you could enter

> A>HELP DIRS EXAMPLES

To see the main explanation (the format and purpose) of the REN command, you would enter

> A>HELP REN

Some of the explanations run longer than 22 lines. HELP will display 22 lines then display "Press ENTER to continue." When you have read the first 22 lines, press the Enter key and HELP will display the next 22 lines. To avoid the pause, enter [P] as the last part of the command (spacing doesn't matter). The entire explanation will be displayed without pauses. This will be useful if echo printing is on.

(a)   Write a command to display the EXAMPLES subtopic of the ERA topic.

>   A>____

(b)   Change the above command so that the display will not pause after 22 lines.

>   A>____

(c)   Write a command to display the COMMANDS topic without pauses.

>   A>____

— — — — — — — — — —

(a) A>HELP ERA EXAMPLES
(b) A>HELP ERA EXAMPLES [P]
(c) A>HELP COMMANDS [P]

Note: The HELP program uses the HELP.HLP file as well as the HELP.CMD file. If you want to copy the HELP program to another disk, be sure to copy both files. You can copy both by using HELP.* as a generalized file reference for PIP command.

THE NEWDISK COMMAND   *See 13, 1. 1 (13-1)*

14. Before a disk can be used for the first time with CP/M-86 and the Personal Computer, it must be formatted by the computer. Formatting involves checking the disk for defects and setting up the disk directory. Any data previously on the disk will be erased in the process. Formatting can also involve copying the system tracks onto the disk if you wish.

The NEWDISK program formats a disk. To use NEWDISK, enter a command in this format:

> NEWDISK *drivename: option*

The *drivename:*, which is required, names the drive containing the disk to be formatted. If you have two drives, you would normally put the system disk in drive A and the new disk in drive B. If you have only one drive, NEWDISK will tell you when to change disks.

The *option*, also required, must be one of four values: $S $N $DS or $DN. $S means you want the system tracks copied onto the disk, and $N means you don't. $DS means you want to format the disk for a two-sided drive *with* the system tracks, and $DN means you want to format the disk for a two-sided drive *without* the system tracks. (You would use $DS or $DN only if you have a two-sided drive and the disk is a two-sided disk.)

When you want to copy the system tracks to a new disk, the disk in drive A must contain those tracks. In this case, always use B as the target drive, even if you don't have a B drive. CP/M-86 will tell you when to put the "B" disk (the new disk) in drive A if you have a one-drive system.

(a) Write a command to format the disk in drive B for a single-sided drive. Do not copy the system tracks.

A>____

(b) Write a command to format the disk in drive B for a double-sided drive. Copy the system tracks.

A>____

(c) For the preceding command [question (b)] which of the following must be true?

______ A. The disk in drive A must be a system disk.

______ B. The disk in drive B must be blank.

______ C. Drive B must be a double-sided drive.

______ D. The disk in drive B must be a double-sided disk.

______ E. The disk in drive A must be a double-sided disk.

——————————

(a) A>NEWDISK B: $N
(b) A>NEWDISK B: $DS
(c) A, C, and D

15. Let's look at a sample NEWDISK interaction.

```
A>NEWDISK B: $S

NEWDISK vn. n,n date

Disk B will be formatted.

ALL DATA WILL BE ERASED FROM THE DISK.   ①

Is this what you want (y/n)? Y   ②

Disk format in progress.
Formatting Track mm   ③
Verifying Track mm   ④
Format complete.
Press Control-C to exit, or
ENTER to format another disk.   ⑤

A>
```

The circled numbers are explained below.

① NEWDISK always reminds us that the disk will be erased. The terminal beeps when this message is displayed. (If echo printing is on, the printer beeps too.)
② We are required to confirm the command by typing and entering a Y here. If we type N, the command is aborted and we see A> again.
③ Each track number (00–39 or 00–79) is displayed as it is formatted.
④ The tracks are then verified (checked for defaults) in reverse order (39–00 or 79–00).
⑤ To terminate the NEWDISK program, we entered Ctrl-C. If we had wanted to format another disk, we would press Enter.

(a) True or false? If the terminal beeps, NEWDISK found a defect on the disk.

____

(b) Suppose you want to erase and reformat the disk in drive B. NEWDISK types
out these messages:

```
Disk B will be formatted.
ALL DATA WILL BE ERASED FROM THE DISK.
Is this what you want (y/n)?
```

What must you reply to make the program reformat the disk in drive B?

____

(c) Suppose at the end you want to format another disk. How would you
respond to "Press Control-C to exit, or ENTER to format another disk"?

____

— — — — — — — — — —

(a) false—it always beeps when it displays the line ALL DATA WILL BE ERASED
FROM THE DISK; (b) y; (c) press Enter

16. Let's review the new commands you have studied so far.

(a) Write a command to find out the format and function of the NEWDISK
command.

A>____

(b) Assume you have been using the HELP program. Write a command to see
some examples of the NEWDISK command.

HELP>____

(c) Write a command to format the disk in drive B. Make it a singled-sided disk.
It does not need the CP/M-86 system tracks on it.

A>____

(d) How do you terminate the HELP program?

____

(e) How do you terminate the NEWDISK program?

____

————————

(a) A>HELP NEWDISK
(b) HELP>NEWDISK EXAMPLES
(c) A>NEWDISK B: $N
(d) press Enter in response to HELP>
(e) press Ctrl-C when given the choice

THE COPYDISK COMMAND *See 13,2 (13-4)*

17.   Sometimes you will want to make a complete copy of a disk, from track 00 through track 39 (for single-sided disks). You can use the COPYDISK utility to do this. COPYDISK is used primarily to make backup copies of program disks that you buy or create. You should make a backup copy of the CP/M-86 master disk as soon as possible. Then put the master away in a safe place and use only the copy. This way, if you inadvertantly damage your system disk, you won't have to buy a new one.

The COPYDISK program is invoked by the simple command COPYDISK. After that, the program tells you what to do. Here is a sample session.

```
A>COPYDISK
CP/M—86 Full Disk COPY Utility
     Version n.n

Enter Source Disk Drive (A–D) ? A ①

 Destination Disk Drive (A–D) ? B ②

Copying Disk A: to Disk B:
Is this what you want to do (Y/N) ? Y ③
Copy started
Verifying Track 0 ④
Copy completed.

Copy another disk (Y/N) ? N ⑤
COPY program exiting
```

The circled numbers are explained below.

①   The *source* disk drive contains the disk to be copied. We wanted to copy the disk in drive A. (You can change the disk in drive A before pressing Enter at this point if you don't want to copy the disk containing the COPYDISK.CMD file.)

②   The *destination* disk drive contains the disk to receive the copy. It must have been formatted by NEWDISK at some earlier time. Any former contents will be completely destroyed by the COPYDISK program; so be sure to use a disk that doesn't contain any files you want to save. In our case, we put the destination disk in drive B.

③   We must confirm our COPYDISK parameters before the copy operation begins.

④   This is all that shows up on the echo printout, but on the monitor screen you can see that the system reads tracks 39 to 30 from the source disk, writes those tracks on the destination drive, and then verifies them. It then does the same with tracks 29 to 20, 19 to 10, and 9 to 0.

⑤   When you respond N to this question, the COPYDISK program terminates itself.

Suppose you want to copy the disk in B drive to the disk in A drive. This is the only copy you want to make.

(a)   Show the command you would use to invoke COPYDISK.

A>____

(b)   Show your response to this message:

```
CP/M-86 Full Disk COPY Utility
      Version 2.0

Enter Source Disk Drive (A-D)?_____________
```

(c)   Show your response to this message:

```
Destination Disk Drive (A-D)?_____________
```

(d)   Show your response to this message:

```
Copying Disk B: to Disk A:
Is this what you want to do (Y/N) ?_____________
```

(e)   Show your response to this message:

```
Copy completed.

Copy another disk (Y/N) ?_____________
```

(f)   True or false? The destination disk does not need to be formatted (using NEWDISK) since the source disk will be formatted._____________

(g)   Suppose you pay $100 for a new program. What should you do before you use the new disk?

____

————————

(a) A>COPYDISK
(b) B; (c) A; (d) Y; (e) N; (f) false—it must be a formatted disk; (g) make a backup copy of the program disk if the copyright permits it (and read the directions for the new program, of course)

THE FUNCTION COMMAND

18.   The FUNCTION command is used to display the settings for the 20 function keys and to reprogram one or more of those keys.

You invoke the command with the single word FUNCTION. You receive back a display like this:

```
A>FUNCTION
FUNCTION utility, v n.n. date
  F1 : dir<CR>
  F2 : dir b:<CR>
  F3 : stat<CR>
  F4 : stat b:<CR>
  F5 : pip<CR>
  F6 : pip b:=a:*.*[v]
  F7 : stat *.*<CR>
  F8 : stat b: *.*<CR>
  F9 :
 F10 :

Home : <ESC>H
   ↑ : <ESC>A
PgUp :
   ← : <ESC>D
   → : <ESC>C
End  : END
   ↓ : <ESC>B
PgDn :
 Ins :
 Del : <DEL>
Function key?:
```

This display shows the current settings for all 20 function keys. The ones shown here are the CP/M-86 default settings. Every time you boot CP/M-86, these defaults are established. The symbol <CR> means the command terminates with the Enter key signal ("Carriage Return" is another term for that key). Thus, those commands will be executed as soon as you press the function key. You don't need to press the Enter key afterwards. If you press F1, for example, you'll see the directory of the default drive.

F1 to F8 are programmed to CP/M-86 commands. The numeric keypad function keys are programmed for cursor control. That is, they are programmed to move the cursor up, down, left, right, etc., as indicated by the arrows on the keys. These cursor control functions do not apply to the CCP or to any of the CP/M-86 built-in or transient programs. However, they may apply to other transient programs that you write or buy and run under CP/M-86. For example, they would probably work beautifully with a word processor running as a transient program under CP/M-86.

(a) What function key will automatically display the directory of the default drive?___________________ _______________________________

(b) Do you need to press Enter after pressing that function key?____________

(c) What function key will automatically display the directory of drive B?__

(d) Do you need to press Enter after pressing that function key?____________

(e) When you are at CP/M-86 command level, can you press the key labeled ↑ to move the cursor up a row?___________________________________

— — — — — — — — — —

(a) F1; (b) no; (c) F2; (d) no; (e) no—those functions do not work with the CCP

19. Here is the FUNCTION screen again.

```
A>FUNCTION
FUNCTION utility, v 1.0 1/25/82
  F1 : dir<CR>
  F2 : dir b:<CR>
  F3 : stat<CR>
  F4 : stat b:<CR>
  F5 : pip<CR>
  F6 : pip b:=a:*.*[v]
  F7 : stat *.*<CR>
  F8 : stat b:*.*<CR>
  F9 :
 F10 :

Home : <ESC>H
   ↑ : <ESC>A
PgUp :
   ← : <ESC>D
   → : <ESC>C
 End : END
   ↓ : <ESC>B
PgDn :
 Ins :
 Del : <DEL>
Function key?:
```

If you want to change the effect of a function key, you respond to the prompt "Function key?:" by pressing the key you want to program. FUNCTION will display the name of the key and an arrow prompt. For example, suppose you want to program F10 to enter the HELP command. After you press F10, the screen will look like this:

```
Function key?: F10
===>_
```

Then you type the command you want to be executed for that key. If you want the command to be entered automatically every time you press the function key, type Ctrl-G at the end of the command. This puts the <CR> in the command. If you don't want the command to be entered automatically, don't type Ctrl-G. When you hit Enter, FUNCTION will record the new function and give you the chance to program another key. Here's what our screen looks like before we press Enter.

```
FUNCTION utility, v 1.0 1/25/82
  F1 : dir<CR>
  F2 : dir b:<CR>
  F3 : stat<CR>
  F4 : stat b:<CR>
  F5 : pip<CR>
  F6 : pip b:=a:*.*[v]
  F7 : stat *.*<CR>
  F8 : stat b:*.*<CR>
  F9 :
 F10 :

Home : <ESC>H
   ↑ : <ESC>A
PgUp :
   ← :<ESC>D
   → :<ESC>C
 End : END
   ↓ : <ESC>B
PgDn :
 Ins :
 Del : <DEL>
Function key?: F10
-> HELP^G
```

Here's what it looks like after we press Enter:

```
  F1 : dir<CR>
  F2 : dir b:<CR>
  F3 : stat<CR>
  F4 : stat b:<CR>
  F5 : pip<CR>
  F6 : pip b:=a:*.*[v]
  F7 : stat *.*<CR>
  F8 : stat b:*.*<CR>
  F9 :
 F10 : HELP<CR>

Home : <ESC>H
   ↑ :<ESC>A
PgUp :
   ← : <ESC>D
   → : <ESC>C
 End : END
   ↓ : <ESC>D
PgDn :
 Ins :
 Del : <DEL>
Function key?: ^C
```

To terminate the FUNCTION program, we press Ctrl-C. There's no other way out except rebooting, which is not desirable since it would restore all the function keys to their default settings.

Suppose you want to change the setting of F1 so that it always gets the directory of drive A no matter what drive is default. You want the command entered automatically. This is the only change you want to make to the function keys.

(a) What do you enter to invoke the correct program?

A>____

(b) What do you type after "Function key?:"

____

(c) What do you type after ===>?___________________________________

(d) Next you will see "Function key?:" again. What do you type now?

____

— — — — — — — — — — —

(a) A>FUNCTION
(b) press the F1 key
(c) DIR A: Ctrl-G
(d) Ctrl-C [to terminate the FUNCTION program]

20.   The commands for F1 through F10 may have up to 18 characters. (Ctrl-G counts as one character.) The commands for the numeric keypad function keys are limited to four characters. You'll most likely start using those keys when you learn to use the ED program, which has short commands.

(a) What is the length limit on commands for F1 through F10?___________

(b) What is the length limit on commands for the numeric keypad function keys?____

(c) True or false? The default functions for the numeric keypad have no effect under the CCP.____

(d) How do you invoke the FUNCTION program?___________________________

(e) How do you terminate the FUNCTION program?___________________________

(f) What symbol puts a <CR> at the end of a command?___________________

— — — — — — — — — — —

(a) 18 characters; (b) four characters; (c) true; (d) enter the command FUNCTION;
(e) press Ctrl-C; (f) Ctrl-G

THE TOD COMMAND   *See 12.7 (12-6)*

21.   The date and time are always displayed on the status line. After booting, they will invariably be wrong. If you want to correct them, you can use the TOD (time of day) command. You might want to do this so screen prints are documented with the correct date and time. CP/M-86 does not use the date and time for any purpose, so it's not essential to correct them. The time is also not kept accurate by the system.

The command TOD without any operands causes the date and time to be displayed on the line after the command line. This is hardly necessary because they already appear continuously on the status line. The command TOD P causes them to be displayed continuously until any other character key is pressed. (They will continue in the status line nonetheless.)

To change the date and time, enter a command in this format: TOD *date time*. The *date* must be in the format mm/dd/yy. You must include leading zeros, and you cannot omit any one of the three parts; you must provide a month, a day, and a year. The *time* must be in the format hh:mm:ss. Here again you must include leading zeros, and you must provide the hour, the minutes, and the seconds. The hour is coded in the 24-hour system, and so 07 means 7 o'clock in the morning; 7 o'clock in the evening is coded as 19. Midnight is 00, not 24.

When you are setting the date and time, code the time 30 seconds or so ahead of what it really is. After you enter the TOD command, CP/M-86 will tell you to "Press any key to set time." When the time you set rolls around, press any key and CP/M-86 will begin tracking the time from that instant.

Suppose you want to set the date and time for your system. Your trusty chronometer tells you it is March 11, 1990 at 1:06 and 14 seconds p.m. Show the command you would use to set the date and time.

A>____

_ _ _ _ _ _ _ _ _ _ _

we would use A>TOD 03/11/90 13:07:00

Now you have been introduced to all the CP/M-86 transients and you have learned how to use HELP, NEWDISK, COPYDISK, FUNCTION, and TOD. The Self-Test will give you a chance to review and practice what you have learned in this chapter.

Chapter Five Self-Test

1.   Name the command you would use for each of the following operations.
     (Don't code the command.)

   a.   Assign a CP/M-86 command to the F10 key. _______________

   b.   Assemble an 8088 Assembly Language program. _______________

   c.   Specify a communications protocol for a serial port. _______________

   d.   Format a blank disk. _______________

   e.   Create a CMD file from an assembled program. _______________

   f.   Specify a communications speed for a serial port. _______________

   g.   Copy a file from drive A to drive B. _______________

   h.   Copy an entire disk from drive A to drive B. _______________

   i.   Specify the printer attached to serial port #0 to act as the listing device.

   ____

   j.   Debug a program. _______________

2.   Code commands for the following functions.

   a.   Read about the purpose and format of the NEWDISK command.

   A>_______________

   b.   Set the current date to April 15, 1985 and the time to 6 o'clock p.m.

   A>_______________

   c.   Copy the disk on drive A to drive B.

   A>_______________

   d.   Format the disk on drive B to be double-sided with the system tracks.

   A>_______________

   e.   Program function keys F1 through F5.

   A>_______________

   f.   See the EXAMPLES subtopic of the REN topic.

   A>_______________

3. Suppose you have this HELP display:

```
DIRS

FORMAT: DIRS {filespec}

PURPOSE:

      Displays the names of system
(SYS) files in the directory of an
on-line diskette.

Additional topics available:

EXAMPLES

HELP>
```

a. Show the command you would use to see the examples of DIRS.

   HELP>____

b. How would you terminate the HELP program and get back to the CCP

   instead?____

c. Instead, how would you request to see the PROTOCOL topic without
   pauses?

   HELP>____

4. Suppose you are using the NEWDISK program. It displays these messages:

```
Disk B will be formatted.

ALL DATA WILL BE ERASED FROM THE DISK. (beep!)

Is this what you want (y/n) ?
```

a. What should you type if you do want to erase and format disk B?

   ____

b. What should you type if you do NOT want to erase and format disk B?

   ____

Now suppose the disk has been formatted and NEWDISK displays this message:

```
Press Control-C to exit, or
ENTER to format another disk.
```

   c.   What should you type if you want to format another disk?

____

   d.   What should you type if you do NOT want to format another disk?

____

5.   Suppose you are using COPYDISK to copy an entire disk from drive A to drive B. This is the only copy you want to make. Show how you would respond to each of the messages below.

   a.   Enter Source Disk Drive (A-D) ?_______________________________

   b.   Destination Disk Drive (A-D) ?_______________________________

   c.   Copying Disk A: to Disk B:

       Is this what you want to do (Y/N) ?_______________________________

   d.   Copy completed.

       Copy another disk (Y/N) ?_______________________________

6.   Suppose you are using the FUNCTION program to program F9 to display a directory of drive C and F10 to display a directory of drive D. Use automatic entry in both cases. Show how you would respond to each of the messages below.

   a.   Function key?: _______________________________

   b.   ===> _______________________________

   c.   Function key?: _______________________________

   d.   ===> _______________________________

   e.   Function key?: _______________________________

Self-Test Answer Key

1. a. FUNCTION
    b. ASM86
    c. PROTOCOL
    d. NEWDISK
    e. GENCMD
    f. SPEED
    g. PIP
    h. COPYDISK
    i. ASSIGN
    j. DDT86

2. a. A>HELP NEWDISK
    b. A>TOD 04/15/85 18:00:00
    c. A>COPYDISK
    d. A>NEWDISK B: $DS
    e. A>FUNCTION
    f. A>HELP REN EXAMPLES

3. a. HELP>DIRS EXAMPLES (Note: Make sure you included DIRS in this
       command.)
    b. press Enter
    c. HELP>PROTOCOL [P]

4. a. Y
    b. N
    c. Enter
    d. Ctrl-C

5. a. A
    b. B
    c. Y
    d. N

6. a. press F9
    b. DIR C: Ctrl-G
    c. press F10
    d. DIR D: Ctrl-G
    e. Ctrl-C

Suggested Machine Exercise

1. Boot with your system disk.

2. Format two blank disks to be used in drive A. Put the system tracks on both disks.

3. Put labels on each formatted disk and mark that they have been formatted. Also mark the bootable disk in some way. (We put a small "f" in the upper right corner of the labels of disks that are formatted without the system tracks and "fs" in the upper right corner of ones that are formatted with the system tracks.)

4. Back up your CP/M-86 disk onto the formatted disk that contains the system tracks.

5. Label your backup copy appropriately and use a piece of tape to write protect it. (There should be some silver tabs of just the right size included in each box of blank disks.)

6. Put your original CP/M-86 disk away in a safe place and from now on use the backup copy only.

7. Reboot using your backup CP/M-86 disk.

8. Now try using the HELP command.
   a. Read the HELP description of DIR.
   b. Look at the examples of DIR.
   c. Now look at the HELP description of filename.
   d. Look at that same description again, but this time use [P] to suppress the pauses.
   e. Now terminate the HELP program and get back to command level.

9. Try out F1 and F2.

10. Now use FUNCTION to reprogram F1 and F2.
    a. Program F1 to invoke the HELP program. Use automatic entry.
    b. Program F2 to get the directory of drive A. DO NOT use automatic entry.
    c. Terminate FUNCTION and get back to command level.

11. Try out F1 and F2 again. You'll have to press Enter after F2 now or it won't work.

12. Set the date and time to be accurate.

13. Reboot.
    a. What happened to the date and time?
    b. What do F1 and F2 do now?

Continue experimenting with these commands until you feel comfortable with them. Then shut down the system and go on to Chapter Six.

CHAPTER SIX
The STAT Command

This chapter covers the STAT program which you can use to display or change the status of various files and devices. For example, STAT can be used to change the status of a disk from read-write to read-only.

The STAT program has several functions. For disks, STAT can display remaining space, read-write status, and active user numbers. STAT can also be used to display the size of files on the disk. STAT can display or change the read-write status as well as display or change the directory status of files. STAT can also display the characteristics of the disk drives.

When you have finished studying this chapter, you will be able to:

- Write STAT commands to display the status of the various devices.
- Interpret status displays produced by the various STAT functions.
- Write STAT commands to change the read-write status of a disk.
- Write STAT commands to specify read-write and directory attributes for a file.
- Write STAT commands to identify user information on a disk.

DISK STATUS

1. The command STAT, with no operands, displays the read-write (R/W) status and amount of space available on each disk. A typical interaction is

```
A>STAT
A: RW, Free Space:        11k
B: RO, Free Space:       151k
```

If you want to find out the amount of available space on a specific drive, use this command format:

```
STAT d:
```

(a) What command produced this output? _______________________________

```
      A: RO, Free Space:        51k
      B: RW, Free Space:        47k
```

(b) Can you write on the disk in drive A? _______________________________

(c) Can you read the disk in drive A? _______________________________

(d) Can you erase files from the disk in drive A? _______________________________

(e) Can you write on the disk in drive B? _______________________________

(f) Can you read the disk in drive B? _______________________________

(g) Can you erase files from the disk in drive B? _______________________________

(h) How much room is available on disk A? _______________________________

(i) How much room is available on disk B? _______________________________

(j) Suppose you change the disk in drive B? What read-write status does the new disk have? _______ How can you change the status? _______________________________

(k) What command produced this output:

```
      B:R/W, Free Space:  24K
```

_ _ _ _ _ _ _ _ _ _

(a) STAT (with no operand); (b) no; (c) yes; (d) no; (e) yes; (f) yes; (g) yes; (h) 51K bytes; (i) 47K bytes; (j) R/O, Press Ctrl-C or reboot; (k) STAT B:

2. You can assign read-only status to a disk by entering a command in this format:

```
      STAT d:=R/O
```

There is no comparable R/W command. To assign read-write status to a disk, you use Ctrl-C, or reboot.

(a) Write a command to assign read-only status to drive A.

A> _______________________________

(b) How do you return drive A to read-write status again? _______________________________

_ _ _ _ _ _ _ _ _ _

(a) A>STAT A:=R/O
(b) press Ctrl-C or reboot

3. (a) Write a command to display the amount of space available on disk B.

A>____

(b) Write a command to display the read-write status of all drives as well as the amount of available space.

A> ____

(c) Write a command to change drive B to R/O status.

A> ____

(d) What do you type to change all disks to R/W status?_______________

— — — — — — — — — — — —

(a) A>STAT B:
(b) A>STAT
(c) A>STAT B:=R/O
(d) Ctrl-C or reboot

The preceding frames have covered the STAT functions for disk status. STAT also provides several functions for individual files on a disk.

FILE STATUS

4. STAT will display the characteristics of a file. The command format is STAT file-identifier. Here's an example:

```
A>STAT PIP.CMD
Drive A:                          User :  0
Recs   Bytes FCBs Attributes    .Name
  59     8k    1 Dir RW         A:PIP      .CMD
- - - - - - - - - - - - - - - - - - - - - - - -

Total:   8k     1
A: RW, Free Space:        11k
```

The output shows that PIP.CMD contains 59 records, take up 8K bytes, and uses one directory entry. (FCB—file control block—is another term for directory entry.) It also shows the current user number and the free space on the disk.

(a) What command produced the message shown below?

```
Drive B:                            User :  0
 Recs  Bytes FCBs Attributes       Name
  240   30k     2 Dir RW          B:INVENTY .DAT
 - - - - - - - - - - - - - - - - - - - - - - - -

 Total:   30k    2
 B: RW, Free Space:           121k
```

(b) What does "FCB" stand for? _______________________________________

— — — — — — — — — —

(a) STAT B:INVENTY.DAT
(b) file control block (directory entry)

5. In the command STAT file-identifier, the file identifier can be generalized. STAT will list the status of all files on the selected disk that match the general filename and also give the amount of available space on disk. The files will be listed in alphabetical order.

Here's an example:

```
A>STAT *.CMD
 Drive A:                            User :   0
 Recs  Bytes FCBs Attributes       Name
  205   26k    2 Dir RW           A:ASM86    .CMD
   16    2k    1 Dir RW           A:ASSIGN   .CMD
   19    3k    1 Dir RW           A:COPYDISK .CMD
  109   14k    1 Dir RW           A:DDT86    .CMD
   72    9k    1 Dir RW           A:ED       .CMD
   14    2k    1 Dir RW           A.FUNCTION .CMD
   45    6k    1 Dir RW           A:GENCMD   .CMD
   52    7k    1 Dir RW           A:HELP     .CMD
   50    7k    1 Dir RW           A:NEWDISK  .CMD
   59    8k    1 Dir RW           A:PIP      .CMD
   14    2k    1 Dir RW           A:PROTOCOL .CMD
   14    2k    1 Dir RW           A:SPEED    .CMD
   73   10k    1 Dir RW           A:STAT     .CMD
   31    4k    1 Dir RW           A:SUBMIT   .CMD
   21    3k    1 Dir RW           A:TOD      .CMD
 - - - - - - - - - - - - - - - - - - - - - - - -

 Total:  105k   16
 A: RW, Free Space:           11k
```

STAT will also do a cross-check of the file directory and notify you if any files seem to show the same space. (This error happens very rarely. If you ever run into it, you can copy the mixed-up files to other disks, then erase them from the confused disk.)

(a)   In the above example, how many records does ED.CMD contain?

____

(b)   How many directory entries does ASM86 use? ___________________

(c)   How much space is available on the A disk? ___________________

(d)   Write a command to find the status of all files on B disk that start with the letters INV.

A> ____

(e)   Write a command to display the status of all files on A.

A> ____

(f)   Show three different commands to find out the amount of space remaining on A.

A> ____

A> ____

A> ____

____

(a) 72; (b) 2; (c) 11K bytes
(d) A>STAT B:INV?????.* or STAT B:INV*.*
(e) A>STAT *.*
(f) A>STAT A: or A>STAT or A>STAT *.* or A>STAT file-identifier for any file on the disk

6.   You may request a SIZE field in a file status display as shown below:

```
B>STAT *.DAT $SIZE
  Drive B:                                          User :  0
     Size   Recs  Bytes FCBs Attributes        Name
      240    240    30k    2 Dir RW            B:INVENTY .DAT
        1      1     1k    1 Dir RW            B:SECOND  .DAT
- - - - - - - - - - - - - - - - - - - - - - - - - - - - - - -

Total:                   31k    3
B: RW, Free Space:             103k
```

The SIZE field gives the file size in records. It will match the RECS field unless the file is random access. Since the subject of random access files is beyond the scope of this book, the SIZE field will not be discussed further.

(a) To display the SIZE field, what operand do you use? _______________

(b) Is the file SIZE given in bytes or records? _______________

— — — — — — — — — —

(a) $SIZE; (b) records

7. When you create a new file it is assumed to have read-write status. To change the status enter this command:

    STAT file-identifier $R/O

The file identifier may be specific or general. File status is not affected by ^C, as the disk status is.
    To change the status back to read-write, use this command:

    STAT file-identifier $R/W

Notice that at least one space precedes the status operand (R/O or R/W) and that it begins with a dollar sign.
    STAT lists the changed file(s) on the console, as in the example below:

```
STAT HELP.* $R/O

A:HELP     .CMD set to Read Only (RO)
A:HELP     .HLP set to Read Only (RO)
A>
```

(a) When a new file is created what is its status? _______________

(b) Write a command to set the status of A:INVENTY.DAT to read-only.

    A> _______________

(c) How can INVENTY.DAT be reset to read-write status?

    A> _______________

(d) Write a command to set the entire disk on drive B to temporary read-only status.

    A> _______________

(e) Write a command to set all the files on B disk to read-only status.

    A> _______________

————————————

(a) R/W
(b) A>STAT INVENTY.DAT $R/O
(c) STAT INVENTY.DAT $R/W
(d) A>STAT B:=R/O
(e) A>STAT B:*.* $R/O

8. Recall that system status means a file will show up in the system directory (DIRS) but not in the regular directory. Also, system files under user 0 are available to all users. To give a file system status, use this command:

      STAT file-identifier $SYS

To remove system status, use this command:

      STAT file-identifier $DIR

The file identifier can be specific or generalized. STAT will tell you which filenames were set by the command to SYS or DIR, as shown below:

```
A>STAT S*.* $SYS

A:SPEED    .CMD set to System (Sys)
A:SUBMIT   .CMD set to System (Sys)
A:STAT     .CMD set to System (Sys)
A>
```

(a) Write a command to make A:PIP.CMD a system file.

    A> ____

(b) Write a command to make all CMD files on disk B system files.

    A> ____

(c) Write a command to make all files on A system files.

    A> ____

————————————

(a) A>STAT PIP.CMD $SYS
(b) A>STAT B:*.CMD $SYS
(c) A>STAT *.* $SYS

9. The preceding section has discussed the various STAT options for file status. The general command format is

STAT file-identifier [$R/O $R/W $SYS $DIR $SIZE]

You may use more than one operand in one STAT command. Thus, you can assign the HELP files to system and read-only status by A>STAT HELP.* $SYS $R/O. If you use no status operands, the status of the file is displayed. The $SIZE operand causes the SIZE to be displayed along with the status.

(a) Write a command to display the status of B:SORT.CMD.

A> ____

(b) Rewrite the command in (a) to include the SIZE field in the display.

A> ____

(c) Write a command to display the status of all files on A disk that start with INV.

A> ____

(d) What will the display from (c) tell you?

______ A. The number of bytes in the files

______ B. The number of bytes remaining on the disk

______ C. The read-write status of the files

______ D. The system status of the files

______ E. Files for other user numbers starting with INV

(e) Write a command to make all files on B disk system files.

A> ____

(f) Write a command to make all CMD files on A disk read-only.

A> ____

— — — — — — — — — — — —

(a) A>STAT B:SORT.CMD
(b) A>STAT B:SORT.CMD $SIZE
(c) A>STAT INV*.*
(d) A, B, C, D
(e) A>STAT B:*.* $SYS
(f) A>STAT *.CMD $R/O

USER STATUS

10. The command STAT d:USR: causes the current user number to be displayed. It also tells you what user numbers are linked to files on the active disk. Here's an example:

```
B>STAT USR:

B: Active User :  1
B: Active Files:  0  1  2  5
```

The display tells you that you're working as user 1. The B disk contains files belonging to users, 0, 1, 2, and 5.

(a) What command obtained the output shown below? A> ___________________

```
A: Active User :  3
A: Active Files:  0  3  13  15
```

(b) According to the above output, what's your current user number? _____

(c) What users have files on the active disk? _______________________________

———————————

(a) STAT USR:
(b) 3; (c) 0, 3, 13, and 15

11. STAT USR: can be combined with DIR and DIRS to identify the user numbers of all files on a disk. The following listing shows you how.

```
A>STAT USER
A: Active User :   3
A: Active Files:   0   3   13   15

A>dir
A: STAT      CMD
A>dirs

NON-SYSTEM FILE(S) EXIST
A>user 0
A>dir
A: HELP      HLP
A>dirs

NON-SYSTEM FILE(S) EXIST
A>user 13
A>dir
A: HELP      HLP
A>dirs

NON-SYSTEM FILE(S) EXIST
A>user 15
A>dir

SYSTEM FILE(S) EXIST
A> dirs
A: CPM       SYS
A>
```

STAT USR: listed all the user numbers on the file—in this case 0, 3, 13, and 15. Then we displayed the regular and system directories under each user number.

(a) Suppose you forget what user number you're currently using. What command should you enter? A> ____

(b) Suppose you're looking for DUMP.CMD on disk A and you don't know what user number to use. You do know it is a system file. What procedure would you use to find the user linked to DUMP.CMD?

____

____

____

____

____

—————————

(a) A>STAT USR:
(b) First, use STAT USR: to find out what user numbers are active. Then use DIRS under each active user number until you find the file you want.

DISK CHARACTERISTICS

12.   The command STAT d:DSK: will display the characteristics of the disk in the specified drive. If the drivename is omitted, all drives that have been accessed since the last boot or reboot are shown.
   Here's an example:

```
A>STAT A:DSK:

         A: Drive Characteristics
     1,248: 128 Byte Record Capacity
       156: Kilobyte Drive  Capacity
        64: 32 Byte  Directory Entries
        64: Checked  Directory Entries
       128: 128 Byte Records / Directory Entry
         8: 128 Byte Records / Block
        32: 128 Byte Records / Track
         1: Reserved Tracks
```

   The drive shown above has the capacity for 1248 records (each record is 128 bytes long); 156K bytes; 64 directory entries; 128 records for each directory entry; 8 records per block; 32 records per track; and 1 reserved track.
   "Checked directory entries" tells how many directory entries your system will check to see if a new disk has been installed on the drive without using Ctrl-C. The system usually checks all the directory entries for floppy disks. If any different entries are found since the last time CP/M-86 checked, the disk is made R/O.
   You probably won't use this command very often as the information doesn't change unless you change your disk hardware.

(a) Write a command to give you the capacity of your drive A.

   A> ____

(b) Write a command to give you the capacity of all your drives.

   A> ____

—————————

(a) A>STAT A:DSK:
(b) A>STAT DSK:

STAT FUNCTION KEYS

13.   Here is the function key list again.

```
FUNCTION utility, v 1.0  1/25/82
  F1 : dir<CR>
  F2 : dir b:<CR>
  F3 : stat<CR>
  F4 : stat b:<CR>
  F5 : pip<CR>
  F6 : pip b:=a:*.*[v]
  F7 : stat *.*<CR>
  F8 : stat b:*.*<CR>
  F9 :
 F10 :

Home : <ESC>H
   ↑ : <ESC>A
PgUp :
   ← : <ESC>D
   → : <ESC>C
 End : END
   ↓ : <ESC>B
PgDn :
 Ins :
 Del : <DEL>
```

(a) Which function key will give you the status of the default drive? ______

(b) Which function key will give you the status of drive B? __________

(c) Which function key will give you the status of all files on the default drive?

____

(d) Which function key will give you the status of all files on drive B? _____

— — — — — — — — — — —

(a) F3; (b) F4; (c) F7; (d) F8

Chapter Six Self-Test

This Self-Test will help you determine if you have mastered the objectives of this chapter. Answer each question to the best of your ability, then check your answers in the answer key at the end of the test.

1.   Briefly describe what the STAT program does.

   ____

   ____

   ____

   ____

2.   Examine the following interaction.

```
A>STAT
STAT?
A>_
```

   What's wrong? _______________________________________

   ____

3.   Write the appropriate command for each of the following STAT functions.

   a.   Display the number of bytes available on disk A. (Use the most efficient method.)

   A> ____

   b.   Make disk B read-only.

   A> ____

   c.   Display the characteristics of all CMD files on disk A.

   A> ____

   d.   Make disk B read-write.

   A> ____

   e.   Display the read-write status of disk B.

   A> ____

4.   Write the appropriate command for each of the following STAT functions.

   a.   Make PIP.CMD a system file.

   A> ____

b.   Make INVENTY.PRN read-only.

A> ____

c.   Display the read-write status of SORT.CMD.

A> ____

d.   Display your current user number.

A> ____

e.   Display the characteristics of all disk drives.

A> ____

5.   Write a command to find out all the user numbers on B disk.

B> ____

6.   The response to your command in question 5 is

```
B:ACTIVE USER :   1
B:ACTIVE FILES:   0   1
```

Write a sequence of commands to display directories of all nonsystem files on this disk.

B> ____

B> ____

B> ____

B> ____

7.   (Optional.) You have learned enough facts to write a sequence of commands to erase all the files from question 6. This problem is different because you can't erase a file with R/O status. See if you can put them all together. (Assume that there is a STAT.CMD for user 0 and another STAT.CMD for user 1. Also assume there are no system files on the disk.)

B> ____

B> ____

B> ____

B> ____

B> ____

B> ____

Self-Test Answer Key

Compare your answers to the Self-Test with the correct answers given below. If all your answers are correct you are ready to go on to the next chapter.

1. Your answer should include these points:
    * Display device status
    * Change device status

2. The system can't find the STAT.CMD file on disk A for your user number.

3. a. A>STAT A:
    b. A>STAT B:=R/O
    c. A>STAT *.CMD
    d. ^C
    e. A>STAT

4. a. A>STAT PIP.CMD $SYS
    b. A>STAT INVENTY.PRN $R/O
    c. A>STAT SORT.CMD
    d. A>STAT USR:
    e. A>STAT DSK:

5. B>STAT USR:

6. B>DIR
    B>USER 0
    B>DIR

7. (Optional.) You need to give all files read-write status before you can erase them. In our solution, we erase user 0 files and then switch to user 1. The last step erases all remaining files.

    B>STAT *.* $R/W
    B>ERA *.*
    B>USER 1
    B>STAT *.* $R/W
    B>ERA *.*

Suggested Machine Exercise

1. Boot with your backup system disk.
2. If you have a line printer, turn on echo print.
3. Display the status of both drives. (Try F3 and F4.)
4. Make the A disk R/O.
5. Display a directory of the A disk.
6. Try to erase one of the files on the A disk. What happens? You should get a BDOS error message. Do you remember what to do now? (Type any character.)
7. Display the status of STAT.CMD.
8. Display the status of all CMD files on the A disk.
9. Display a directory for your user number.
10. Make STAT.CMD a system file.
11. Display a new directory. Notice that STAT.CMD does not appear.
12. Display the characteristics of all disk drives on your system.
13. Display the current user status.
14. Change your user number.
15. Display the user status again. (STAT will work because you made it a system file under user 0.)

This completes the suggested machine exercise for STAT. When you are ready, go on to Chapter Seven.

The PIP Command

One of the most useful CP/M-86 transient programs is the Peripheral Interchange Program (PIP). PIP is used to transfer files from one device to another. You can copy a file from disk to disk, or from disk to a peripheral device such as CON: or LST:. You can also transfer files from an input device such as CON: or RDR: to any other device. Thus, PIP is one way to create a new disk file under CP/M-86. (You'll be learning the more common way in later chapters.) PIP can be used to copy the CP/M-86 programs from one disk to another so you'll need PIP whenever you initialize a disk. You'll find you use PIP more and more as you become more familiar with it.

PIP can also combine files into a new file and modify the new file as it is copied.

After you complete this chapter, you will be able to:

- Write a PIP command to copy a single file.
- Use the continuing PIP format to copy a series of files.
- Use generalized names to copy a collection of files using either PIP format.
- Use PIP parameters to specify changes in the new file(s).
- Use PIP to concatenate files.
- Place a copy of PIP.CMD in a new user area.

THE BASIC PIP COMMAND

1.   The CP/M-86 utility program that you use to copy files is called PIP—the Peripheral Interchange Program. With PIP you can copy a file onto the same or another disk, changing its name if you wish. You can also combine files or copy several files with one command. By using codes you can modify the copied file, such as putting it in all upper case letters or adding line numbers.

Name the CP/M-86 program that accomplishes each function below.

(a) Make a copy of a file on another disk._________________________________

(b) Display the amount of space left on a disk._____________________________

(c) Format a disk and copy the system tracks to it._________________________

(d) Copy a data file, convert it to uppercase, and rename it._______________

_ _ _ _ _ _ _ _ _ _ _

(a) PIP; (b) STAT; (c) NEWDISK; (d) PIP

2. To use PIP to copy files, you must have the PIP.CMD file on an installed disk and available to your user number. Later in this chapter we'll see how to make PIP available to your user number. A drive prefix can be used with the PIP command to access the program from any drive.

When you copy a file with PIP, the original file is not altered. It remains in the previous location after the PIP operation. Any requested changes will appear in the new version, which may have the same name if it is on a different disk or user number.

The general form of the basic PIP command is

    PIP destination-file=source-file[parameters]

Any changes to the file are specified as parameters. We'll cover those later in the chapter. First we'll examine the basic copy function of PIP.

(a) Suppose you have the PIP.CMD file on drive A, but B is the default drive. How can you use PIP without switching the default drive?

    B>____

(b) Here is a valid PIP command:

    A>PIP PROGRAM.FOR=SAMPLE.FOR

Which file(s) exist(s) before the PIP command is entered?

____

(c) Which file(s) exist(s) after the PIP program is executed?

____

(d) What will be the difference between the two files?

____

— — — — — — — — — — —

(a) B>A:PIP
(b) SAMPLE.FOR
(c) PROGRAM.FOR and SAMPLE.FOR
(d) just the name

3. A specific file can be copied on the same disk or to another disk. The drivename can be part of either or both filenames in the PIP command. Whenever the drivename is omitted, the default drive is assumed for that file. For example, in this command:

A>B:PIP STOCK.MOD=B:STOCK.MED

PIP.CMD is on drive B, as is the source file STOCK.MED. The destination file is to be created on drive A, the default drive. For each example below, give the drive on which the PIP program and the source file are located, and identify the drive where the destination file is to be created.

(a) B>A:PIP A:PAY.FOR=PAY.FOR

PIP______ source______ destination______

(b) A>PIP PAY.FOR=PAYROLL.FOR

PIP______ source______ destination______

(c) C>A:PIP B:PAY.CMD=PAY.CMD

PIP______ source______ destination______

(d) B>PIP A:PAY.DAT=B:PAY.PER

PIP______ source______ destination______

— — — — — — — — — — —

(a) A, B, A; (b) A, A, A; (c) A, C, B; (d) B, B, A

4. Write commands to perform these operations. PIP.CMD resides on the default disk.

(a) Copy a file named PEOPLE.DAT from drive A to drive B. Don't change the name.

A>____

(b) Copy the same file as in (a), but change the name to EMPLOYEE.LST.

A>____

(c) Copy file SALARY.HST from drive B to drive A. Don't change the name.

   A>____

(d) Make another copy of SALARY.HST on drive A. Name the new copy SALARY2.HST.

   A>____

————————————————

(a) A>PIP B:PEOPLE.DAT=PEOPLE.DAT (or =A:PEOPLE.DAT)
(b) A>PIP B:EMPLOYEE.LST=PEOPLE.DAT (or =A:PEOPLE.DAT)
(c) A>PIP SALARY.HST=B:SALARY.HST (or A:SALARY.HST=)
(d) A>PIP SALARY2.HST=SALARY.HST

ABBREVIATING PIP

5.   Abbreviated PIP commands can be used when you are copying files without changing names. This may happen when you are copying from one disk to another or from one user number to another. You can use any of these forms:

    PIP specific-file-identifier=d:
    PIP d1:specific-file-identifier=d2:
    PIP d:=file-identifier
    PIP d1:=d2:file-identifier

Answer (a) in the preceding frame could be written PIP B:PEOPLE.DAT=A: or B:=PEOPLE.DAT and would have the same effect. Answer (c) could be written PIP A:=B:SALARY.HST or SALARY.HST=B: instead. The file named SALARY.HST on disk B would be copied to the A disk and given the same name.

   Write the shortest possible commands to copy these files. PIP.CMD is on disk A.

(a) Make a copy of file B:MONEY.XYZ on disk A. Change the name to MONEY.BAK.

   A>____

(b) Copy the file B:MONEY.XYZ, but don't change the file identifier.

   A>____

(c) Make a copy of file ANTHRO.REC from drive A onto drive B. Don't change the name.

   A>____

———————————

(a) A>PIP MONEY.BAK=B:MONEY.XYZ
(b) A>PIP MONEY.XYZ=B: or A:=B:MONEY.XYZ
(c) A>PIP B:ANTHRO.REC=A: or B:=ANTHRO.REC

COPYING MULTIPLE FILES

6. We've been talking about copying one file at a time by coding a specific file identifier in the PIP command. CP/M-86 also lets you specify a generalized file identifier as a source file causing several files to be copied. The rules for coding general file identifiers for use in PIP are the same as those for use in other CP/M-86 commands. You can use * to fill out one part of the name with any characters or ? to fill a specific position with any character.

When you use a generalized file identifier, the PIP command must take this form:

    PIP d:=generalized-file-identifier
    PIP d1:=d2:generalized-file-identifier

The command PIP B:=*.CMD will result in the copy of all files from the default disk that have filetype CMD to disk B. No names are changed. If CMD files already exist on disk B with the same names, they are replaced. When you specify a generalized file identifier in a PIP command, PIP displays the specific names of the files it copies so that you know the results.

Assume PIP is on disk A.

(a) Write a command to copy all files of filetype FOR from disk A to disk B.

  A>____

(b) Write a command to copy all files from disk B to disk C.

  A>____

(c) Write a command to copy all files whose filenames begin with A2 from disk B to disk A.

  A>____

———————————

(a) A>PIP B:=*.FOR
(b) A>PIP C:=B:*.*
(c) A>PIP A:=B:A2*.*

CONCATENATING FILES

7.   PIP can also be used to combine several source files into a single destination file. This process is called *concatenation*. Here is the command format for concatenation:

      PIP destination=source1,source2,source3,etc.

The destination file identifier is written as usual. The source file identifiers you wish to combine are typed and separated by commas. All the names must be specific; no wildcards are allowed. Each source file is processed separately so each can be on a different disk if necessary. CP/M-86 assumes that each source file to be concatenated contains text (ASCII) characters and ends with a Ctrl-Z character. This is the standard symbol to mark the end of an ASCII file. (You'll learn how to create this type of file in Chapter Eight.) The end-of-file characters, except for the last, are eliminated in the destination file; so it winds up with only one end-of-file character, which is in the proper position.

(a)   Write a command to combine files ONE.ASM and TWO.ASM into a new file, NEW.ASM, on the same drive.

      A>____

(b)   Write a command to combine these three files: STOCK.ONE, STOCK.TWO and STOCK.THR, from drive B into a file MASTER.STK on drive A.

      A>____

(c)   How many end-of-file marks will be in MASTER.STK after the three source files are concatenated?____

— — — — — — — — — —

(a) A>PIP NEW.ASM=ONE.ASM,TWO.ASM
(b) A>PIP MASTER.STK=B:STOCK.ONE,B:STOCK.TWO,B:STOCK.THR [Did you put the drivename before each source filename? In this example, it's necessary or PIP will look on disk A for the file.]
(c) only one

8.   When files are concatenated under CP/M-86, they are combined in the order you specify. If the destination file existed before the command, it is replaced with the new file. The source files are unchanged in most cases, but it's possible to specify the destination as one of the source files. For example:

      PIP MASTER.STK=MASTER.STK,STOCK.ADD

In this case, the files MASTER.STK and STOCK.ADD will be combined into a single file which will replace the original MASTER.STK.

(a) Write a command to combine files FIX.ONE from disk A, disk B, and disk C into a file FIX.ALL on disk B.

   A>____

(b) Write a command to combine the three source files from (a) into the original source file from disk B.

   B>____

(c) In which of the above cases [(a) or (b)] are the source files unchanged after the concatenation?

____

— — — — — — — — — —

(a) A>PIP B:FIX.ALL=FIX.ONE,B:FIX.ONE,C:FIX.ONE
(b) A>PIP B:FIX.ONE=FIX.ONE,B:FIX.ONE,C:FIX.ONE
(c) in (a)

NONDISK DEVICES

9. PIP also allows you to transfer files to and from physical and logical devices that are attached to your system. The source devices you can use are:

CON:	The console input device. This is your keyboard unless you have changed it with the ASSIGN command.
AXI:	An auxiliary input device. If you have one, it must be connected to one of your serial or parallel ports and assigned to AXI: by the ASSIGN command.

The destination devices you can use are:

CON:	Your console output device. This is your monitor unless you have changed it with the ASSIGN command.
AXO:	An auxiliary output device. If you have one, it must be connected to one of your serial or parallel ports and assigned to AXO: by the ASSIGN command.
LST:	Your listing device. This is the same device that receives the output of echo and screen printing.
PRN:	The same as the listing device, but PIP formats the output; tabs are expanded to every eight column, lines are numbered, and a new page is started every 60 lines.

   Some additional device names are also available but aren't used much by nonprogrammers.

You can combine file and device names in the same PIP command. For example, PIP CON:=B:STUDENT.DAT will copy the file STUDENT.DAT from disk B to the console.

(a) Write a command to concatenate files A:FILE.ONE and B:FILE.TWO and copy them to the list device. Use line numbers, tab expansion, and paging.

A>____

(b) Perform the operation in (a) above, but don't use line numbers, tab expansion, or paging.

A>____

(c) Copy file NEW.ASM from disk B to the console device.

A>____

— — — — — — — — — —

(a) A>PIP PRN:=FILE.ONE,B:FILE.TWO
(b) A>PIP LST:=FILE.ONE,B:FILE.TWO
(c) A>PIP CON:=B:NEW.ASM

RESULTS OF PIP

10. When you enter a PIP command, CP/M-86 copies the file. You may be able to hear disk movements or changes. When the operation is complete you'll receive the command prompt again.

If you enter a command that is invalid for some reason, you'll see "INVALID FORMAT," "FILE NOT FOUND," "NO FILE," or some other error message. The copy will not even begin if the command is not correctly formed.

If you do a copy without parameters, you will not be able to interrupt PIP once the copy has begun without rebooting. If one device is not a disk, or if you use one of the PIP parameters, you *may* be able to interrupt the output using Ctrl-S and restart it with any character except Ctrl-C. You may be able to abort the command by typing any character except Ctrl-S. PIP responds with

```
ERROR: USER ABORTED
A>_
```

What is indicated by each of these interactions?

(a) A>PIP FIX.ONE=FIX.BAK

PIP?

A>_

____

(b)   A>PIP FIX.ONE=FIX.BAK

ERROR: FILE NOT FOUND - A:FIX.BAK

A>_

(c)   A>PIP FIX.ONE,FIX.BAK

ERROR: INVALID FORMAT — ,

A>_

(a) PIP.CMD is not on the A disk for your user number; (b) file FIX.BAK is not on disk A; (c) we need = instead of ,

USING PIP COMMAND LEVEL

11.   We have been discussing the one-line command format of PIP. All of the functions and formats we've covered also work with the other PIP format. If you simply type PIP and press Enter, PIP responds with a PIP prompt (an asterisk) like this:

```
A>PIP
*
```

Now you can enter a command line, just as in an one-line PIP command. When you enter the line, the operation takes place. However, instead of returning you to CP/M-86 at the default drive, the system leaves you in PIP and gives you another PIP prompt. You can continue entering command lines until you don't need PIP anymore. To return to CP/M-86 level simply press Enter when you receive an askerisk (*). You are immediately returned to the CCP.

Here's an example:

```
1.   A>PIP↵
2.   *B:=*.CMD ↵
3.   *B:=*.BAS ↵
4.   * ↵
5.   A>_
```

In line 1, we entered the PIP command with no operand. (The ↵ symbol indicates where we pressed Enter.) PIP displayed the * prompt on line 2. We entered the command to copy all CMD files from the default drive to drive B. PIP did that, then displayed the * prompt on line 3. We entered the command to copy all BAS files from the default drive to drive B. PIP did that, then displayed the * prompt on line 4. We pressed Enter to terminate PIP. The CCP then displayed the CP/M-86 command prompt on line 5.

Suppose you need to copy three files FIX.ONE, FOX.TWO, and FOX.TWI from disk A to disk B. You also need a file B:FOXY.ALL made up of FOX.TWO and FOX.TWI. You'll want to use the multiple-line format.

(a) Write your first entry.

    A>____

(b) Write a command line to copy FIX.ONE

    *____

(c) Write a command line to copy FOX.TWO and FOX.TWI

    *____

(d) Write a command line to create B:FOXY.ALL

    *____

(e) How did you terminate PIP?

    *____

— — — — — — — — — — —

(a) A>PIP
(b) *B:=FIX.ONE
(c) *B:=FIX.TW?
(d) *B:FOXY.ALL=FOX.TWO,FOX.TWI
(e) Enter
[In (d) you could have used the source files on disk B.]

12. The multiple line format of PIP may also be used to copy files on disks that don't contain PIP.CMD. For example, suppose you have disk 1 containing PIP.CMD and disk 2 containing SORT.CMD. You want to copy SORT.CMD to disk 3, which doesn't contain PIP.CMD either. Also, suppose you have only two drives.

First, put disk 1 on drive A, disk 3 on drive B, and enter PIP. CP/M-86 responds:

```
A>PIP
*_
```

Then remove disk 1 from drive A, install disk 2, and enter:

```
*B:=SORT.CMD
```

The copy will be successfully made.

After starting PIP, you cannot write on the disk you changed (it will have R/O status), but you can copy a file from it as that involves only reading from the source disk

Suppose you also want to copy SORT.MSG to disk 3. However, it's on disk 4, which does not contain PIP. If the above PIP session is ongoing, how would you make the copy?

____

____

____

— — — — — — — — — —

put disk 4 in drive A and enter *B:=SORT.MSG

THE PIP PARAMETERS

You have now seen the basic copy functions of PIP. With PIP you can copy one file with a specific file identifier or several files with a generalized name. You've seen how to concatenate files with PIP and how to use both PIP formats. Now we're going to look at the PIP parameters. Each of these has a specific effect on the copy operation.

The PIP command has 19 different parameters that you can use to modify the file being copied. Appendix B includes a complete listing with brief explanations for you to refer to later. We're going to look at the various parameters and see how you can use them as you work with CP/M-86.

13.   One useful parameter is E, which stands for "echo." When you use the E parameter the transferred data is also echoed (or displayed) on the console. This tends to slow down the PIP operation; however, it does show exactly what is being transferred. To use any parameter, enclose it in square brackets [E] immediately following the source file identifier. (You may omit the closing bracket if you wish.)

Which of these commands is correctly formed?

_____   (a)   PIP [E]STOK.ONE=STOK.TWO

_____   (b)   PIP STOK.ONE[E]=STOK.TWO

_____   (c)   PIP STOK.ONE=STOK.TWO[E]

— — — — — — — — — —

(c)

14.   Parameters are available for translating a file into all uppercase letters [U] or all lowercase [L]. The destination file will be all one case or the other, depending on the parameter used.

Parameters can be combined as in this example:

PIP STOK.ONE=STOK.TWO[UE]

The file STOK.TWO will be transferred as STOK.ONE, with all lowercase letters converted to uppercase. STOK.ONE will be echoed on the console. The parameters can be in any order and either uppercase or lowercase letters may be used.

Write commands with parameters to accomplish these operations.

(a)   Copy FILE.X from disk A to disk B. Convert all uppercase letters to lowercase. Don't display it on the console.

A>____

(b)   Copy all files of type SM6 from disk B to disk A. Convert lowercase letters to uppercase. Don't display them on the console.

A>____

(c)   Copy file DEPART.TYM as DEPART.NEW. Convert to all uppercase letters and display the transferred data.

A>____

— — — — — — — — — — — —

(a) PIP B:=A:FILE.X[L]
(b) PIP A:=B:*.SM6[U]
(c) PIP DEPART.NEW=DEPART.TYM[UE] or [EU]

15.   Some parameters can be used only with certain types of files. Only files with alphabetic characters, for example, can be converted to uppercase or lowercase. And only printable characters will make sense on the console. The Dn parameter—delete n characters—only makes sense for certain files. When you specify Dn, any characters that extend beyond column n are deleted. This can be done only with a file containing printable characters. Dn is often used to truncate long lines that are being sent to a narrow printer or console. If a print device has only 40 columns, you might specify [D40], especially if you need to see only the first 40 columns.

(a)   Could you specify D60 for a CMD file?_______________________________

(b)   Write a command to transfer FILE.XY as FILE.AB, convert it to uppercase, delete anything beyond column 50, and echo the result on the console.

A>____

———————————

(a) no—CMD files aren't printable files;
(b) PIP FILE.AB=FILE.XY[UED50] (the parameters can be in any order)

16. You saw earlier that you can PIP a file to the PRN: device with the result that line numbers are added, tabs are expanded to every eighth column, and a page break occurs every 60 lines. With three parameters you can achieve the same effect on LST: or a disk file. If you then TYPE the resulting disk file, the effect will be the same as PIPping it directly to PRN:, but now you also have a copy on disk. Here are the parameters:

N	Add line numbers
Tn	Expand tabs every n columns
Pn	Start a new page every n lines

If you use T without n, tabs are not expanded. If you use P without n, a page break occurs every 60 lines. Therefore a parameter of [NT8P] or [NT8P60] has the same effect as PIPping a file to the PRN: device. Of course, the parameters can be in any sequence.

(a) Convert to lowercase, expand tabs every fourth column.

____

(b) Page after 50 lines, add line numbers, and limit destination file to 80 characters per line.

____

(c) Create a disk file in the same format as PRN: file.

____

———————————

(a) [LT4];
(b) [NP50D80];
(c) [NT8P] or [NT8P60]

17. When line numbers are added with [N], the line number is printed without leading zeros and followed by a colon, like this:

       1:   LINE 1
       2:   LINE 2

If you specify [N2], leading zeros are printed and a tab is inserted following the line number. If the destination is disk, T8 is assumed. If the destination is LST:, the tab setting on the printer is used. In the example below we had the printer tab stop set at 15.

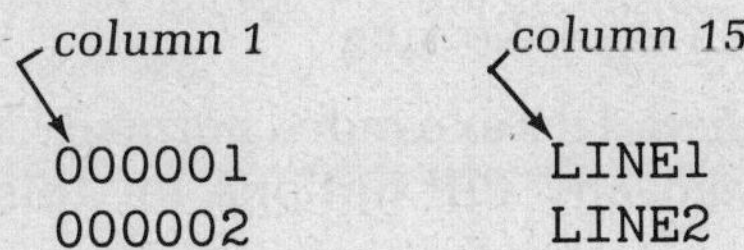

On the standard Personal Computer parallel printer, there are no tab stops and therefore no space appears between the line number and the line.

If you specify [N2Tn], the tabs will be expanded so that the next character begins in column n+1. For [N2T10] the display looks like this:

       column 1   column 11
       000001   LINE1
       000002   LINE2

Don't use E (echo print) with N (number lines). The combination is legal, but the line numbers get mixed up because PIP numbers the lines that are displayed as well as the lines that are stored or listed.

(a) Write the parameter list to number lines in this format:

       1:   RESTORE1
       2:   RESTORE2

* ____

(b) Write the parameter list to number the lines and insert tabs, expanded to

     column 15.____

— — — — — — — — — — — —

(a) [N];
(b) [N2T14] (you can't use N instead of N2 because N does not insert a tab after the line number)

18.   The F parameter is used to filter, or remove, form feeds (page breaks) from a file. Suppose you created a disk file using this parameter list [NT8P50]. Now you want to print it out but you need exactly 54 lines per page. What do you do? You use this command:

> PIP LST:=CURRENT.FIL[FP54]

The F parameter filters all the page breaks from CURRENT.FIL, and P54 inserts new ones every 54 lines. If F and P are in the same parameter list, the existing page breaks are always removed before the new ones are added.

Assume that DOCUMENT.FUL was originally created with these parameters: [N2T8P60]. Write commands to accomplish the following:

(a)   Print DOCUMENT.FUL with line numbers, tabs expanded normally, and 60 lines per page. (*Hint:* You don't need any PIP options for this one.)

    A>____

(b)   Print DOCUMENT.FUL with 48 lines per page.

    A>____

(c)   Print DOCUMENT.FUL with tabs expanded every eight columns and no page breaks.

    A>____

— — — — — — — — — —

(a) PIP LST:=DOCUMENT.FUL (or TYPE DOCUMENT.FUL with echo printing on)
(b) PIP LST:=DOCUMENT.FUL[FP48]
(c) PIP LST:=DOCUMENT.FUL[F]
[Remember that the order of parameters and whether you use capital (uppercase) or small (lowercase) letters is unimportant. You may use parameters that are in effect anyway, such as T8 for question (c) above.]

19.   We've covered quite a few PIP parameters for use with files that contain character data. As a review, give the parameter you'd use to accomplish each of these functions:

(a)   Display transferred data on the console. ___________________________

(b)   Expand tabs every six columns. ___________________________

(c)   Insert a page break every 50 lines. ___________________________

(d)   Remove all previous page breaks. ___________________________

(e)   Convert lowercase letters to uppercase. ___________________________

(f)   Convert uppercase letters to lowercase. ___________________________

(g)   Add line numbers to a file. ___________________________________

(h)   PIP only the first 72 characters of each line. ___________________

— — — — — — — — — — —

(a) E; (b) T6; (c) P50; (d) F; (e) U; (f) L; (g) N or N2; (h) D72

20.   Sometimes you may not want to copy an entire file in a PIP operation. You can use the S and Q parameters to tell PIP to start (S) and quit (Q) copying at certain points. If you use S, but not Q, the copy will start at the point you specify and run to the end of file. If you use Q, but not S, the copy will start at the beginning of the file and quit where you specify. If you use both, you can determine both the first and last parts of the new file.

You specify the starting or quitting location as a string of characters. Suppose you want to start copying where the word SUBROUTINE first appears. You code the parameter like this:

        [SSUBROUTINE<Ctrl-Z>]

Where we show <Ctrl-Z>, you should type the single Ctrl-Z character, not the eight characters that are shown. To quit where the next RETURN appears, you'd modify the parameter to look like this:

        [SSUBROUTINE<Ctrl-Z>QRETURN<Ctrl-Z>]

Notice that each string is terminated with Ctrl-Z. Uppercase and lowercase letters in the string must exactly match in the file.

Write parameters to indicate the following:

(a)   Begin the copy operation where CHAPTER 2 occurs.

____

(b)   The last part of the new file should be ;END.

____

(c)   Assume the text of this frame is a file. You want to copy the third sentence onto a separate file.

____

— — — — — — — — — — —

(a) [SCHAPTER 2<Ctrl-Z>]
(b) [Q;END<Ctrl-Z>]
(c) [SIf you<Ctrl-Z>Qfile.<Ctrl-Z>]

21.   You might have coded more words for question (c) of the preceding frame. That's perfectly all right. The copy will start at the first "If you" and end after the next "file." it encounters.

The S and Q strings are converted to uppercase in the one-line PIP format, when you enter the entire command at CP/M-86 command level. So whenever you are dealing with uppercase and lowercase, as in the above example, you need to use PIP command level.

The spacing, punctuation, and capitalization must be exact for PIP to identify a string.

Suppose you want to PIP a file to contain the second paragraph of this frame. Which of the following will accomplish that?

_____ (a)   A>PIP LINES.45=FRAME.21[SThe S<Ctrl-Z>QPIP command level.<Ctrl-Z>]

_____ (b)   A>PIP
*LINES.45=FRAME.21[SThe S<Ctrl-Z>Qcommand level<Ctrl-Z>]

_____ (c)   A>PIP
*LINES.45=FRAME.21[SThe S<Ctrl-Z>QPIP command level.<Ctrl-Z>]

_ _ _ _ _ _ _ _ _ _ _

(c) [The strings in (a) would be converted to uppercase and wouldn't match; (b) would copy only the first sentence

22.   You may want to copy a file from another user area to the active one. You do this with the Gn parameter where n specifies the user number of the source file. If you are working under user 3, for example, and have PIP.CMD under user 3 (or as a system file under user 0), you can copy files from other user areas. You might use PIP A:=STAT.CMD[G0] to copy the STAT program from user area 0 into your current area. If STAT is a system file under user 0, you also need to specify parameter R. Then STAT will be a system file after it is copied as well. You can also *send* a file to another user number. You do this by putting [Gn] after the destination file identifier. This is the only case where the destination file identifier can have a PIP parameter. For example, suppose you are user 0 and you want to copy PIP.CMD to user 3. You would code:

A>PIP PIP.CMD[G3]=PIP.CMD

Assume you are user number 5 and you have PIP available to you. Write commands to accomplish the following:

(a) Copy the file ASM.CMD from user area 1 to user area 5.

A>____

(b) Copy all nonsystem files from user 5 to user area 4.

A>____

(c) Copy all files, including file system files, from user 4 to user 5.

A>____

(d) Copy MY.DAT from user 5 to user 2 on drive B.

A>____

— — — — — — — — — — —

(a) A>PIP A:=ASM.CMD[G1]
(b) A>PIP A:[G4]=*.*
(c) A>PIP A:=*.*[G4R]
(d) A>PIP B:[G2]=MY.DAT

23. Under normal conditions PIP will not overlay a file that is set to R/O status. If you attempt this, CP/M-86 tells you:

    DESTINATION IS R/O, DELETE (Y/N)?

If you enter Y, the file will be overlaid with the copied file of the same name. If you enter N or any other character, the file is not transferred and CP/M-86 says **NOT DELETED**. If you want PIP to go ahead and overlay without asking you each time, you can use the W parameter. With the W parameter, any R/O files will be deleted and replaced with new ones.
Consider this command:

    A>PIP A:=*.*[G3RW]

(a) What is the general effect?_______________________________________

____

(b) Suppose you are user 1 and the only file in your area is PIP.CMD, which is set to R/O. If user area 3 contains PIP.CMD as a system file, will it be

transferred?_______ Will your PIP.CMD be overlaid?_______________

(c) How could you modify the command above so that the system files will be copied from user 3, but CP/M-86 will ask before overlaying any R/O files?

— — — — — — — — — —

(a) copy all files from user area 3 to the active user number; (b) yes, yes; (c) PIP
A:=*.* [G3R] (eliminate the W)

Several PIP parameters are used only in special cases: B, O, H, I, and Z. We
won't cover them in this book. Another parameter [V can be used with all PIP
operations, but it tends to double the time PIP takes. When you specify [V, the
copied data is verified before the copy is completed. If you will be writing your
own programs, or using non-ASCII files, you may want to look up these additional parameters in Appendix B.

24.   Write PIP commands with parameters required to accomplish the following:

(a)   Copy file RILEY.WIL to the list device. Number each line, expand tabs to
      every fifth position, change the page breaks to every 70 lines.

      A>____

(b)   Print the portion of RILEY.WIL that begins "To my son" and ends
      "Washington, D.C.". These must not be interpreted as uppercase. Use the
      PRN: device.

      A>____

      *____

(c)   How do you return control to the CCP?

      ____

— — — — — — — — — —

(a) A>PIP LST:=RILEY.WIL[NT5FP70]
(b) A>PIP
    *PRN:=RILEY.WIL[STo my son<Ctrl-Z>QWashington, D.C.<Ctrl-Z>]
(c) Enter

25.   Here is the FUNCTION list again.

```
A>function
FUNCTION utility, v 1.0 1/25/82
  F1 : dir<CR>
  F2 : dir b:<CR>
  F3 : stat<CR>
  F4 : stat b:<CR>
  F5 : pip<CR>
  F6 : pip b: =a:*.*[v]
  F7 : stat *.*<CR>
  F8 : stat b:*.*<CR>
  F9 :
 F10 :

Home : <ESC>H
   ↑ : <ESC>A
PgUp :
   ← : <ESC>D
   → : <ESC>C
 End : END
   ↓ : <ESC>B
PgDn :
 Ins :
 Del : <DEL>
```

(a)   What key would you press to enter PIP command level?_________________

(b)   Do you need to press Enter after pressing that key?_______________

(c)   What key would you press to copy all the files from disk A to disk B?__

(d)   Do you need to press Enter after pressing that key?________________

— — — — — — — — — —

(a) F5; (b) no; (c)F6; (d) yes

Chapter Seven Self-Test

1. Write the command to copy CHAP7.EX to the same disk under the name CHAP7.TST.

   A>____

2. Write the command to copy CHAP7.EX from disk A to disk B. Keep the same name.

   A>____

3. Write the command to copy all files from disk to disk B.

   A>____

4. Write the command to copy all files starting with the characters CHAP7 from disk B to disk A.
   A>____

5. Write the command to combine CHAP7.P1 and CHAP7.P2 as CHAP7.PRN. All three files are on disk A.

   A>____

6. Write the command to combine CHAP7 from disk B with CH7.TST and CH7.EX from disk A. The new file should replace CHAP7 on disk B. Echo the transferred data on the console.

   A>____

7. Write the command to display CHAP7.PRN on the console, translating all letters to lowercase.

   A>____

8. Write the command to print CHAP7.PRN on the printer with line numbers, tabs expanded to the eighth column, and page breaks every 60 lines.

   A>____

9. Write the command to print CHAP7.PRN on the printer, with line numbers. Delete everything after column 40.

   A>____

10. Write the commands to print CHAP7.PRN on the console, from "1." through "concatenation.".

    A>____

    *____

11. Write the command to print CHAP7.PRN on the printer, remove existing form feeds, and start a new page every 45 lines.

    A>____

12. Write the command to copy CHAP7.PRN from user 0 to user 3. Assume that you are starting as user 0.

    A>____

13. Write the command to copy all files, including system files, from user 0 to user 3. Don't replace any existing files if they have R/O status. Assume you are user 3.

    A>____

14. Change your command from question 13 so that existing R/O files are automatically replaced.

    A>____

15. Starting from user 0, write the command to copy PIP.CMD from user 0 to user 4.

    A>____

Self-Test Answer Key

1. A>PIP CHAP7.TST=CHAP7.EX
2. A>PIP B:=CHAP7.EX
3. A>PIP B:=*.*
4. A>PIP A:=B:CHAP7*.*
5. A>PIP CHAP7.PRN=CHAP7.P1,CHAP7.P2
6. A>PIP B:CHAP7=B:CHAP7,CH7.TST,CH7.EX[E]
7. A>PIP CON:=CHAP7.PRN[L]
8. A>PIP PRN:=CHAP7.PRN or PIP LST:=CHAP7.PRN[NT8P60]
9. A>PIP LST:=CHAP7.PRN[ND40]
10. A>PIP
    *CON:=CHAP7.PRN[S1.<Ctrl-Z>Qconcatenation.<Ctrl-Z>]
11. A>PIP LST:=CHAP7.PRN[FP45]
12. A>PIP A:[G3]=CHAP7.PRN
13. A>PIP A:=*.*[G0R]
14. A>IP A:=*.*[G0RW]
15. PIP A:[G4]=PIP.CMD

Suggested Machine Exercise

1. Boot using your backup system disk. Put a blank, formatted disk in drive B.

2. Create a new file on drive B by PIPping from CON: to B:TRY.0.
   a. Enter PIP B:TRY.0=CON:
   b. The cursor will move to the next line. Type a few words.
   c. Press Enter.
   d. Type another line and press Enter.
   e. Type as many lines as you like this way.
   f. Enter Ctrl-Z to end the file and terminate the PIP command.

3. PIP the file to TRY.1 on the same disk.

4. Check the disk directory for TRY.1.

5. PIP the file to TRY.2 (same disk) and have it echo on the console.

6. PIP the file to TRY.3 using line numbering and tabs every 10th column.

7. TYPE TRY.3 to see the effect.

8. PIP the file to TRY.4 using lowercase translation. Use echo to see the effect.

Try using the multiple line format for the next three commands.

9. PIP the file to the console.

10. PIP the file to PRN:

11. PIP the file to LST: and compare the results.

12. Try making two new files, TRY.5 and TRY.6, from parts of the source file. Use echo to see the effect.

13. Concatenate TRY.5 and TRY.6 into TRY.7. TYPE TRY.7 to see the effect.

14. Try some faulty commands. How about PIP A:=TRY.9? Or try PIP B: = TRY.6.

15. Transfer the file to a different user number.

16. Switch to that user number and get a directory. It should show the file you put there.

17. Give the last file R/O status.

18. Now try to replace the file. PIP it from user 0 to the new user number. You should get a "read only" message.

19. Erase all the various files you have created in this exercise.

Now go on to Chapter Eight.

CHAPTER EIGHT

Introduction to ED

The ED program is the CP/M-86 text editor. You use ED to type new files and store them on disk. You also use ED to change existing files.

When you enter d>ED filename, you go to the ED command level. You can then enter a wide variety of ED commands. You interact with ED in the same fashion that you interact with the CCP. In this chapter, and the following two, you will learn the ED commands and how to use them. However, if you will be using any word processor, don't bother with ED; skip to Chapter Eleven.

In Chapter Eight you'll learn how to initiate ED. You'll study some general ED facilities such as line numbering. Then you'll learn how to create a new text file under ED and how to save that file on disk. In your Suggested Machine Exercise you'll actually create a new file.

When you have finished this chapter, you will be able to:

- Initiate ED for a new file.
- Turn line numbering on and off.
- Turn uppercase translation on and off.
- Initiate ED's insert level.
- Type and store data in memory.
- Use the CP/M-86 control characters under ED.
- Terminate insert level.
- Terminate ED.
- State the meaning of various ED messages.

TEXT EDITING

1. ED is a text editor. You use it to create and change text files. ED is not used with CMD files, but you can use it to create source program files.

To create a file you type it on your console. ED stores it in the memory and then when you're ready, stores it on the disk.

To change a file, ED moves the file from disk into the memory. You can then use editing commands to delete, insert, and/or replace data. When you're ready, ED stores the changed file back on the disk again. ED also keeps a backup copy of the original file, just in case you change your mind.

Which of the following can ED be used for?

_____ (a)   Create a new CMD file.

_____ (b)   Create a new data file.

_____ (c)   Change an existing data file.

_____ (d)   Change the system tracks.

— — — — — — — — — — —

(b) and (c) [we didn't discuss (d), but by now you should know that you can access the system tracks only with NEWDISK]

2.   ED is a *character editor*. This means that you work on one character at a time. Characters are grouped together to form *lines*. To ED, a line is any string of characters terminated by carriage return and line feed characters. Both the carriage return and the line feed, in that order, must be present to mark the end of an ED line.

In this book we'll abbreviate carriage return as <CR> and line feed as <LF>. When you press the Enter key, it generates a <CR>.

When you're creating a new file with ED, you type a line at your terminal, then press Enter. ED stores the <CR> character and *automatically adds the <LF> character*. Both the <CR> and <LF> are displayed on your terminal. You won't see "<CR><LF>". You'll see the effect—the cursor moves to the beginning of a new line.

(a)   What is a line?

_____ A.   80 characters on the console.

_____ B.   Any string of data in memory terminated by <CR>.

_____ C.   Any string of data in memory terminated by <CR><LF>.

(b)   According to the above definition, could a line contain zero characters (not counting the <CR> and <LF>)? _______________________________

(c)   Could it contain 6000 characters? _______________________________

(d)   When you're typing data under ED, how do you mark the end of a line?

____

(e)   When you press Enter, what does ED store in memory?

____

(f)   What will be displayed on your console? _______________________________

____

— — — — — — — — — —

(a) C; (b) yes; (c) yes (but it may look funny when displayed on your terminal or printed on your line printer); (d) press Enter; (e) <CR><LF>; (f) the cursor moves to the beginning of the next line

3.   Suppose you're working with ED, and main memory contains this data:

```
THE ACME INSURANCE CORPORATION<CR><LF>CORDIALLY
INVITES YOU TO ATTEND A<CR><LF>NON-SMOKER'S
SEMINAR<CR><LF>DOWNTOWN PLAZA HOTEL<CR><LF>FEB.
4 AT 6 PM<CR><LF><CR><LF>R.S.V.P.<CR><LF>
```

This file contains seven lines. The next to the last line is empty—it contains no data.

Now let's store this file on the disk and display it using TYPE. The display will look like this:

```
THE ACME INSURANCE CORPORATION
CORDIALLY INVITES YOU TO ATTEND A
NON-SMOKER'S SEMINAR
DOWNTOWN PLAZA HOTEL
FEB. 4 AT 6 PM

R.S.V.P.
```

Suppose you're working with ED and main memory contains this data:

```
NAME:<CR><LF>ADDRESS:<CF><LF><CR><LF>
<CR><LF>PHONE:<CR><LF>
```

(a)   How many lines does this file contain? ______________________________

(b)   If you TYPE it out, what will it look like?

— — — — — — — — — —

(a) five
(b) NAME:
    ADDRESS:

    PHONE:

THE CHARACTER POINTER

4.   As you fill memory with text data, ED keeps track of your position in memory. Imagine that ED maintains a pointer that always indicates your current position in memory. We call this the *character pointer* and show it like this:

        THE ACME INSURANCE COMPANY<CR><LF>
                                          ^

The mark (˄) indicates the character pointer. In our example it's at the beginning of a new line. This character pointer does not show up on your screen or your printouts. It's an imaginary pointer.

  The location of the character pointer is very important. All the ED commands operate on the current character or the current line. For example, if you enter the command

        D

ED will delete the character after the pointer. (The asterisk is the ED command prompt.) If you enter the command

        -D

ED will delete the character before the pointer.
  If you enter the command

        K

ED will delete (Kill) the data from the character pointer to the end of the line.
  Suppose main memory looks like this:

        3142D NO. 2 PENCILS BOX/12<CR><LF>
                                 ^

(a) Where is the character pointer?

    _______ A.   At the end of the line

    _______ B.   At the beginning of the next line

    _______ C.   At the beginning of this line

(b) Suppose you enter this command:

    -D

What will the line look like in memory?

_____ A. 3142D NO . 2 PENCILS BOX/12$_\wedge$<LF>

_____ B. 3142D NO . 2 PENCILS BOX/1$_\wedge$<CR><LF>

_____ C. $_\wedge$<CR><LF>

_____ D. No change to line

(c) Suppose you enter this command:

    -K

What do you suppose the line will look like in memory?

_____ A. 3142D NO . 2 PENCILS BOX/12$_\wedge$<LF>

_____ B. 3142D NO . 2 PENCILS BOX/1$_\wedge$<CR><LF>

_____ C. $_\wedge$<CR><LF>

_____ D. No change to line

____

(a) A; (b) B; (c) C

5.   ED includes a set of commands to move the character pointer wherever you want. You can move it forward or backward, by character or by line. You can also jump it to the beginning or end of the file in memory. There are also commands to display the current line so you can figure out where the character pointer is. You'll be learning how to use all these commands in a later chapter, when you learn how to change an existing file.

For now, let's review what you've learned about character editing and the character pointer.

```
FOURSCORE AND SEVEN YEARS AGO<CR><LF>OUR FATHERS
BROUGHT FORTH ON THIS CONTINENT<CR><LF>A NEW NAT
ION CONCEIVED IN LIBERTY<CR<LF>
```

(a) How many lines are in the above example? _______________________

(b) Where is the character pointer? _______________________

(c) If you entered this command:

    D

What effect would it have? _______________________

(d) If you entered this command:

    K

What effect would it have? _______________________

— — — — — — — — — —

(a) 3; (b) at the beginning of the third line; (c) the "A" would be deleted; (d) the third line would be killed

LINE NUMBERING

6. As a further aid in keeping track of lines, you can use ED's line numbering facility. If you want, ED will display a 5-digit number at the beginning of each line on your console.

The line numbers are not stored with your data in memory. They just appear on the console when you display lines.

A typical display might look like this:

```
00001:  PAUL JONES
00002:  16 MAPLE ST.
00003:  POWAY, CA 92064
```

Which of the following statements are true?

_______ (a) Line numbers are always displayed.

_______ (b) Line numbering is optional.

_______ (c) Line numbers are stored with the data in the file.

_______ (d) Line numbers are displayed but not stored.

_ _ _ _ _ _ _ _ _ _

(b) and (d)

7. Line numbering is turned on by the command:

   V

It's turned off by the command:

   -V

Line numbering is automatically on when you initiate ED. If you don't want to use the numbers you have to turn them off with the -V command.

(a) Show the ED command to turn line numbering on. _____

(b) Show the ED command to turn line numbering off. _____

(c) Will line numbering be on or off when you initiate ED? _____________

_ _ _ _ _ _ _ _ _ _

(a) V; (b) -V; (c) on

UPPERCASE TRANSLATION

8. You have already learned how to use the CapsLock key to translate all letters to uppercase. Another way is to use the U command under ED. If you choose to use ED's uppercase translation feature leave the CapsLock key alone. Enter the ED command:

   U

ED will translate letters *after* they're sent from the terminal. On your display you'll see the lowercase letters, but uppercase letters are stored in memory. When you print or display the file, the capital letters will appear.
   To turn uppercase translation off again, enter:

   -U

(a) What's the ED command to turn on uppercase translation? _____

(b) What's the ED command to turn off uppercase translation? _____

_ _ _ _ _ _ _ _ _ _

(a) U; (b) -U

Now that you have learned about character editing, the character pointer, line numbering, and uppercase translation, you're ready to begin learning how to use ED. In this chapter we'll show you how to create a new file using ED. In later chapters, you'll learn to edit existing files.

THE SETUP

9. In order to create a new file, you're going to need two basic things: the ED.CMD file and some available disk space for the new file. In this chapter we'll assume that both files will be on the same disk.

Suppose that a STAT of disk A shows that ED.CMD is a system file with R/O status. There are 7K bytes left on A.

(a)   Can you use the ED program to create a new file on this disk? __________

(b)   Suppose you plan to create a file containing 10K bytes. Can you do it on this

disk?____

— — — — — — — — — —

(a) yes; (b) no, you'll need a disk with more available space

10.   Let's assume you want to build a file name MAILIST.DOC on the default disk, under user 0.

To assign MAILIST.DOC to user number 0, you must create it under user number 0. Therefore, you must have ED available under user 0.

Suppose you're logged on as user 0. What's the best way to find out if ED.CMD is on the disk for user 0?

A>____

— — — — — — — — — —

A>DIR ED.CMD will either show the directory entry if it's a directory file or "SYSTEM FILE(S) EXIST" if it's a system file.

11.   The command to call ED and name the file is

      d>ED d:specific-file-identifier

For our file, we would enter

      A>ED MAILIST.DOC

The ED program is loaded into the memory and given control. It searches the disk directory for the file identifier. If found, it assumes you want to change the file. If not found, ED assumes you want to create the file and opens up two new directory entries on the disk. One directory entry is for the specific file identifier and the other is for a temporary work file named filename.$$$. ED will later erase the $$$ file.

(a) Suppose you want to create a file on disk A named INDEX.DAT. Show the command you would enter.

A> ____

(b) Suppose ED.CMD is on disk A but you want to create the file on disk B. Show the command you would enter.

A> ____

(c) How many directory entries must there be space for on a disk to create a new file with ED? ____

(d) After you enter the command in (a) above, what new files will ED put on disk A? Name the files. ____

(e) Can you use a generalized filename with ED?_____

_ _ _ _ _ _ _ _ _ _ _

(a) A>ED INDEX.DAT
(b) A>ED B:INDEX.DAT or A>B: followed by B>A:ED INDEX.DAT
(c) two; (d) INDEX.DAT and INDEX.$$$; (e) no

12.   When we enter A>ED MAILIST.DOC, we want the response shown below:

```
NEW FILE
      : *_
```

The first line tells us that we have specified a file identifier that does not appear in the directory. Therefore, ED starts a new file.

The second line shows the line number, then gives the ED command prompt, *. The line number indicates the line containing the character pointer. When it's blank, the character pointer is at the beginning of a nonexistent line.

(a) What is the ED command prompt? ____

(b) In the transaction below, show the command to turn line numbering off.

```
A>ED MAILIST.DOC
NEW FILE
      : *____
```

— — — — — — — — — —

(a) an asterisk (*); (b) *-V

13. It's usually pretty simple to get ED started on a new file, but there are some things that can go wrong.

If ED isn't available, you'll get this message:

```
ED?
```

If the selected disk has read/only status, you'll get this message:

```
BDOS ERR ON A: R/O_
```

If the file already exists, a number of different things could happen. If the file has R/W and DIR status, ED assumes you want to change the file and gives this response:

```
A>ED INDEX.DOC
  : *_
```

When you see this response, you know that ED has found a file with the name you gave.

If the existing file has R/O status, you'll get this response:

```
* *FILE IS READ/ONLY **
      : *_
```

This warning message tells you that you can read the file under ED, but you can't make any changes to it. You'll need to terminate ED and try again using a different file identifier.

Suppose you want to create a new file named PRACTICE.DOC. You have this display:

```
A>ED PRACTICE.DOC
 ** FILE IS READ/ONLY **
      : *_
```

(a) What program level are you now at—CCP or ED? _______________________

(b) Can you now begin typing your new file? _____ Why or why not? _____

____

(c) How can you get out of this situation? _____________________________

____

Suppose instead you have this display.

```
A>ED PRACTICE.DOC
     : *_
```

(d)   What program level are you now at: CCP or ED? ________________________

(e)   Can you now begin typing your new file? _______ Why or why not? _______

____

Suppose you try to put your new file on B disk and get this response:

```
A>ED B:PRACTICE.DOC
BDOS ERROR ON B:   R/O
```

(f)   What's wrong? ____

____

(g)   How can you get out of this situation? _______________________________

____

____

____

— — — — — — — — — —

(a) ED; (b) no; there already is a PRACTICE.DOC file on the A disk; (c) one way is
to use Ctrl-C to terminate ED, then start over using another file identifier; (d) ED;
(e) no; the response indicates that there already is a PRACTICE.DOC file on disk
A because ED didn't say NEW FILE; (f) disk B has read-only status so ED can't
write a new directory entry; (g) press Ctrl-C and then disk B will have R/W status
(Note: Before you continue, make sure you know why B disk had R/O status—
was it an accident or intentional?)

USING LINE NUMBERS

14.   Let's assume that you have successfully opened a new file under ED and
you have this display:

```
A>ED MAILIST.DOC
NEW FILE
     : *_
```

Before you go any further, you should decide whether you want to use line
numbering or not. Remember that the line numbers don't get stored in the file.
ED displays them to help you move around in the file while you're editing it.

Even though they aren't needed when typing a new file, we tend to leave them on—except when we want eight more characters on each display line. The line numbers take up space, leaving a 72 character display on the terminal. If we're entering 80-character records, we'll turn line numbering off so that we can get a complete record on one line.

If you want to leave line numbering on, don't do anything. If you want to turn it off, enter -V. The system will respond like this:

```
   :  *–V
 *_
```

Suppose you have this display:

```
A>ED MAILIST.DOC
       :  *_
```

(a) Is line numbering on or off? _____

(b) Show the command to change it. *_____

———————————————

(a) on; (b) *-V

INSERT LEVEL

15. Now that you've decided about line numbering you're ready to begin entering data. As far as ED is concerned, you're going to *insert* data into the file.

The ED command for insert is I or i. If you use the capital letter I, all inserted letters will be translated to uppercase before being stored. If you use the lowercase i, all letters will be stored exactly as you type them.

If you follow the command immediately with <CR>, you'll invoke ED's insert level. At insert level, ED will *store all characters* that you type until it encounters the terminator character, Ctrl-Z.

Up until now, all the CP/M-86 commands you've learned have been terminated by <CR>. This is not true with the I command. If you press Enter when inserting data, ED stores and displays <CR><LF>, giving you a new line. But you are still in insert level. To end the insert level, you must type Ctrl-Z.

(a) Show the ED command to initiate the insert level with uppercase translation. _____

(b) How do you terminate insert level and get back to ED command level? _____

(c) In insert level, what effect does Enter have? _______________________

____

(d) Show the ED command to initiate insert level without uppercase translation. *_____

———————————

(a) *I; (b) type Ctrl-Z; (c) inserts <CR><LF> in the data (and ends the line); (d) *i

16.   Now let's walk through an example of inserting data. We'll start at the
CP/M-86 command level.

```
A>ED  INDEX.DOC
NEW  FILE
      : *_
```

You're now at the ED command level and ready to enter insert mode.

```
   : *I
   1: _
```

From the line number, you can see that ED is ready to receive line 1. With line
numbering off, the lack of any prompt tells you that you're at the insert level and
ED is ready to receive data.
   Suppose you have this display:

```
A>ED MAILIST.DOC
NEW  FILE
      : *-V
*I
   _
```

(a) What level are you at now? ____

(b) Can you begin typing data for MAILIST.DOC? _______________________

In the display below, show what ED's response will be.

```
A>ED MAILIST.DOC
 NEW FILE
      : *I
```

(c) ____

——————————

(a) ED insert level; (b) yes; (c) 1: _

17. Once in insert mode, all you do is type the data you want to put in the file. What happens when you reach the end of a line and press Enter? ED stores a carriage return <CR> and line feed <LF> in memory and displays them on your terminal. Therefore you start a new line in your file.

On your terminal, it looks like this:

```
1: THE THORSON COMPANY<CR>
2: _
```

Main memory now looks like this:

```
THE THORSON COMPANY<CR><LF>^
```

Suppose you have this interaction:

```
A>ED MAILIST.DOC<CR>
     : *I<CR>
   1:  JUDI N. FERNANDEZ<CR>
   2:  _
```

(a) What level are you now at? _______________________________________

(b) Can you enter an ED command? _______________________________________

(c) Can you continue entering data in MAILIST.DOC? _______________________

— — — — — — — — — —

(a) ED insert level; (b) no—that is, you can type the command but ED will treat it as data for MAILIST.DOC; (c) yes

```
A>ED MAILIST.DOC<CR>
NEW FILE
     : *I<CR>
   1:  THE THORSON COMPANY<CR>
   2:  16 MAPLE ST.<CR>
   3:  SAN DIEGO, CA  92117<CR>
   4:  <CR>
   5:  DUOTECH, INC.<CR>
   6:  9968 HIBERT ST.<CR>
   7:  SAN DIEGO, CA  92131<CR>
   8:  ^Z
   8: *_
```

Figure 8.1   Display to Create MAILIST.DOC

18.   You just keep on typing lines until you've finished your file. Figure 8.1
shows the display for creating MAILIST.DOC.

If you make any typing errors, don't forget about the CP/M-86 control characters. You can use them to correct the errors. Use Backspace or Ctrl-H to backspace
and erase one character. Ctrl-X will delete the line you're working on.

So far, you have not learned to backspace without erasing characters as you go.
For example, if you want to correct the error in this line:

        NOW 19 THE TIME_

you'll have to backspace:

        NOW I_

and retype the remainder of the line:

        NOW IS THE TIME_

Another way to correct the line would be to store it as is, then correct it from
ED command level later on. You'll learn the details of using D and K in the next
chapter.

(a)   Suppose you have this interaction:

        1:   THE THORSON COMPANY<CR>
        2:   16 MAPLR_

How can you change the "R" to "E"? ________________________________

____

(b)   How can you delete the line you're working on? __________________

— — — — — — — — — —

(a) use either Ctrl-H or Backspace to delete the "R" then type the "E"; (b) Ctrl-X

TABBING

19.   When you are inserting data, you may want to use the CP/M-86 tab character Ctrl-I. This character causes a tab to be inserted in your stored data and
immediately displayed. Ctrl-I is a CP/M-86 control character. It will work at any
level of CP/M-86. We haven't discussed it before because you usually only use
tabbing with ED.

On your console CP/M-86 puts tab stops in columns 1, 9, 17, 25, ... Every time
you type Ctrl-I, the cursor will jump to the next tab stop. If your echo printer is
on, the same tab stops are used on the printer.

There is no way to change the tab stops without changing the CP/M-86 program. However, you have learned how to use PIP's Tn parameter to change the tab stops to every nth column when PIPping a file.

(a)   What columns are tab stops under ED? ________________________

(b)   How do you tab to the next stop? ________________________

(c)   Can you set your own tab stops? ________________________

— — — — — — — — — —

(a) 1, 9, 17, 25, . . . ; (b) type Ctrl-I; (c) not unless you modify the CP/M-86 program

20.   Suppose you want to store lines that are longer than the line on your console. For example, the monochrome display has 80-character lines but you may want to type data records containing 100 or more characters.

You can store any line length you want by not pressing Enter until you're ready to end the line. When you reach the end of a console line, the cursor will move to the beginning of a new line automatically.

Why would you want a long line length? If you're working with both a line printer and video terminal, your printer may have a longer line. Also, if you're preparing input data records for a computer program, the program dictates the length of the record.

Can you store lines in memory that are longer than your console line? ______ If

so, explain how. ________________________

____

— — — — — — — — — —

yes, just keep typing and finish the data for a line before you press Enter

21.   Now you've seen how to get into insert level and how to type the data you want. When your file has been typed, use Ctrl-Z to terminate the insert. You'll be returned to ED command level. For an example of a complete session, refer to Figure 8.1 again.

Show the commands you would use to build a new file in memory named PRACTIC.DAT which would contain this data: THIS IS A PRACTICE FILE. Use line numbering.

(a)   A> ________________________

      NEW FILE

(b)   : * ____

(c)   1: ________________________

— — — — — — — — — — —

(a) ED PRACTICE.DAT; (b) I; (c) THIS IS A PRACTICE FILE. <Ctrl-Z>

22.   When you terminate insert level, your data is stored in memory but is not on the disk yet. You must tell ED to write it on the disk. There are several different commands you could use.

> E — Writes the data on the disk and terminates ED. You go back to CP/M-86 command level. This is the *normal* exit.
>
> H — Writes the data on the disk, but restarts ED for the same file. You can now change the file you've just created.
>
> W — Writes the first line from memory to the $$$ file (or sometimes to another part of memory). The line is eliminated from memory and the other lines are moved up. W may be preceded by a number indicating how many lines should be moved. Thus, 25W means write 25 lines. A pound sign (#) can be used to mean 65535, which usually means "all". Thus, #W means write all lines.

The H command can be used when you have finished creating a file and you want to go back and edit it. H is often used to make a backup copy in case of a power failure. The W command is used to empty memory and keep going. You'll need to do this if your file is larger than the space available in your memory. However, H immediately writes the data on disk, whereas W may simply move it to another part of memory.

(a)   Suppose you've just finished typing a new file and you want to save it on disk and terminate ED. What command would you enter? * _____

(b)   What response would you expect from the above command?

> _____ A. *_
>
> _____ B. A>_

(c)   Suppose you've just finished typing a new file but it contains a lot of mistakes. You want to save it on disk and then correct it using ED commands. What command would you enter? * _____

(d)   What response would you expect from the above command?

> _____ A. *_
>
> _____ B. A>_

(e) Suppose you're at insert level and have the display shown below. Fill in the commands to empty memory and then continue to insert more lines. (*Hint:* You'll need several commands to do this.)

```
24:    GOODTIME POOL SUPPLY
25:    118B ST.
26:    TUCSON, AZ  85730_
```

____

____

(f) Suppose you've been working about half an hour typing new lines. You're concerned that a power failure might cause a loss of all the data in memory. You want to save your current work on disk, then keep on editing. (This is standard practice at many places—it's done every ½ hour or so.) Which command is better, *H or *#W? _____ Why? ______________________

____

____

____

(a) *E (b) B; (c) *H (d) A; (e) you need to get to ED command level, save the file, then reenter insert level—Ctrl-Z followed by *#W or *26W, followed by *I; (f) *H is better because it will actually write the data on disk. *#W may only move it to another part of memory where it could also be lost

23. Sometimes you decide to cancel the work that you've done without saving it on disk. ED allows you to do this also. There are several ways.

> Ctrl-C—The system reboot will work from the ED command level.
> Q—This ED command works similarly to Ctrl-C, but asks you this question first:

$$Q - (Y/N)?\_$$

If you really mean to quit, type Y. If you entered Q by mistake, type N.

> O—This ED command means to return to the original file. The editing work you've done is eliminated from memory but you stay in ED and can start over.

The major difference between Ctrl-C and Q is what happens to your files. If you use Ctrl-C, ED has no chance to close out the files. They both remain in the disk directory. However, neither one contains data, even if you've used the W command. With Q, ED takes the time to close the files properly. The $$$ file is eliminated and the "filename" file contains lines written by W. (This is different from the situation if you were editing an existing file. You'll learn about that later.)

(a) Suppose you have this display:

```
A>ED MAILIST.DOC
NEW FILE
      : *Q

Q - (Y/N)?_
```

If you really mean to quit, what should you do? _______________________

(b) Following the above interaction, suppose you get a directory of the A disk. What files would be included in the directory?

_____ A. MAILIST.DOC

_____ B. MAILIST.$$$

_____ C. Neither of these

(c) Suppose you have this interaction:

```
A>ED MAILIST.DOC
NEW FILE
      : *<Ctrl-C>

A>DIR
```

What files would be included in the directory?

_____ A. MAILIST.DOC

_____ B. MAILIST.$$$

_____ C. Neither of these

(d) Suppose you have the display shown below. You then realize that you're entering the wrong data. You want to eliminate the two lines and start over. Show the commands you'll need.

```
A>ED MAILIST.DOC
NEW FILE
      : *I
    1:   ANDREW W. JORDAN
    2:   25 AMES ROAD_
```

____

____

____

— — — — — — — — — —

(a) type Y; (b) A; (c) A and B; (d) Ctrl-Z followed by *O followed by *I

24. You may be wondering whether the CP/M-86 control characters work with ED. At the ED command level, indicated by the * prompt, all the control characters work. At the insert level, indicated by no prompt, only some of the control characters work. The following chart indicates when the control characters work.

Ctrl	Command	Insert
H	X	X
I	X	X
X	X	X
Z	X	X
P	X	
C	X	
S	X	

If you want echo printing on while you're in insert mode, use it at ED command level before you enter the I command. You'll have to go back to ED command level to turn it off again.

Which of the following CP/M-86 control characters don't work at the ED insert level?

_____ (a) Ctrl-P   _____ (e) Ctrl-H

_____ (b) Ctrl-I   _____ (f) Ctrl-X

_____ (c) Ctrl-C   _____ (g) Ctrl-S

_____ (d) Ctrl-Z

— — — — — — — — — —

(a), (c), and (g)

ED ERROR MESSAGES

25. You've already seen some of the error messages you can get when you try to open a new file. Now we'll show you some other error messages.

If you enter an invalid ED command, you'll get a message in this format:

    BREAK "s" AT x

The "s" is a symbol indicating the type of error. The x is the character ED "broke" on. We usually get this message when we forget to enter insert level and type data on command level. The interaction might look like this:

```
A>ED EXAMPLE.DOC
NEW FILE
      : *WHO ARE YOU?
BREAK "?" AT H
      : *I
     1:  WHO ARE YOU?
```

This BREAK message is questioning the H that follows W, since W is a valid ED command.

If you enter more data than memory can hold, you'll get this message: BREAK ">" AT x. The greater than (">") sign means your data is greater than the memory size. Use the W command to move lines from memory to the disk. Then you can continue adding data in memory.

If you finish your file in memory and it's too long to fit on the disk, you'll get this message:

```
DISK OR DIRECTORY FULL
A>_
```

This is disastrous because you've been kicked out of ED without saving your data. There is no way you can recover the data without extrememly sophisticated recovery programs. You can prevent this error by checking the disk space with STAT *before* you initiate ED. Estimate the size of your new file. Then make sure the disk has at least twice that amout of space available to allow for the $$$ and backup files.

(a) Suppose you have this interaction:

```
    250:   THE COST OF THE PROJECT WILL BE $25,000.<CR>
BREAK ">" AT C
      : *_
```

What's wrong? ____

How can you get out of this error condition? ________________________

____

(b) Suppose you have this interaction:

```
A>ED MEMO.DOC
NEW FILE
      : *MEMO TO ALL STAFF
BREAK "?" AT E
      : *
```

What's wrong? ____

How can you get out of this error condition?________________________

____

(c) Suppose you have this interaction:

```
1000:             THE END^Z
1000:  *E
DISK OR DIRECTORY FULL
A>
```

What's wrong? ____

How can you get out of this error condition? ______________________

____

How can you prevent it? ______________________________________

____

____

— — — — — — — — — —

(a) memory is full; use #W to empty memory; (b) unrecognizable ED command; use I to enter insert mode; (c) the new file didn't fit on the disk; you can't remedy this situation; you've lost the file. Always use STAT to check available space before starting a new file

In this chapter you have seen how to initiate ED, select line numbering and uppercase translation, enter insert level, insert data while making corrections as necessary, save the data on disk, and terminate the edit session.

The format of command to initiate ED is

d>ED d:specific-file-identifier

The ED command prompt is a single asterisk (*), which may be preceded by a line number indicating the current position of the character pointer.

The ED commands that you have learned are:

```
     U—turns uppercase translation on
    -U—turns uppercase translation off (default)
     V—turns line numbers on (default)
    -V—turns line numbers off
     I—initiates insert level (i for upper- and lowercase)
     E—ends ED and saves file
    nW—writes n lines from memory to $$$ file; # is used for 65535
     Q—quits ED with no editing saved
     O—returns to original file
```

At the ED command level, all the CP/M-86 control characters work as usual. At the ED insert level, these control characters work:

Ctrl-I—tab
Ctrl-H—backspace
Ctrl-X—backspace to beginning of line
Ctrl-Z—terminate insert

You'll practice using these commands in the Self-Test and Suggested Machine Exercise.

Chapter Eight Self-Test

1. Show the CP/M-86 command to initiate ED for a new file named CHAPTER8.ST
   A> ____

2. Identify the meaning of each of the following responses.

   _____a.   ** FILE IS READ/ONLY **   1.   The file already exists.
             : *_   2.   ED is ready to create a new
   _____b.   NEW FILE   file.
             : *_   3.   ED.CMD file is not available.
                                         4.   The disk has read-only status
   _____c.   : *_   and you can't put a new file
   _____d.   BDOS ERROR ON A: R/O   on it.

   _____e.   ED?
             A>_

3. Show the command to turn line numbering on. * ____________________

4. Show the command to turn line numbering off. * ____________________

5. Show the command to turn uppercase translation on. * ____________________

6. Show the command to turn uppercase translation off. * ____________________

7. Show the command to initiate insert level. * ____________________

8. Show the command to terminate insert level. * ____________________

9. On your display screen, how can you tell the difference between insert level

   and ED command level? ____

   ____

10. What's the control character for tabbing? _____

11. Which of these control characters work at the insert level and which work at the command level? Label I (insert), C (command), or B (both).

    _____ a. Ctrl-P

    _____ b. Ctrl-I

    _____ c. Ctrl-S

    _____ d. Ctrl-H

    _____ e. Ctrl-X

    _____ f. Ctrl-C

12. Show the command to terminate ED and save the data on disk. *_______

13. Show the command that will terminate ED but not save the data on disk.
    *_____

14. Show the command to save all lines in the $$$ file and keep going. *_____

15. Show the command to save the data on disk and restart ED for the same file.
    *_____

16. Show the command to return to the origianl file and start over. *_____

17. Which of the following errors is unrecoverable?

    _____ a. BREAK "#" AT T

    _____ b. DISK OR DIRECTORY FULL

    _____ c. BREAK ">" AT D

18. How can the above error be prevented? _______________________________

    ____

19. What types of files can ED create?

    _____ a. CMD

    _____ b. text

Self-Test Answer Key

1. A>ED CHAPTER8.ST
2. a. 1
   b. 2
   c. 1
   d. 4
   e. 3
3. *V
4. *-V
5. *U
6. *-U
7. *I
8. Ctrl-Z
9. ED command level is indicated by the command prompt, *. Insert level has no prompt.
10. Ctrl-P
11. a. C
    b. B
    c. C
    d. B
    e. B
    f. C
12. *E
13. *Q
14. *#W
15. *H
16. *O
17. b
18. Check available disk space with STAT before initiating ED.
19. b

Suggested Machine Exercise

In this exercise you'll practice creating several short files. In steps 1 to 11 you'll create a short file containing this message:

> THIS IS A PRACTICE FILE.
> I AM EXPERIMENTING WITH ED.

1. Boot from a disk that contains STAT.CMD and ED.CMD. (Create the disk if you have to by PIPping STAT.CMD and ED.CMD to a blank, bootable disk.)
2. Use STAT to check the available space on your disk. You'll need at least 2K.
3. Repeat steps 1 and 2 until you have a disk with plenty of space.
4. Initiate ED for the PRACTICE.1 file.
5. Turn on echo printing.
6. Initiate insert level.
7. Type the file. Correct typing errors as you go.
8. Terminate insert level.
9. Save the file and terminate ED.
10. Check your disk directory. You should see PRACTICE 1 there.
11. TYPE PRACTICE.1. (Don't erase it.)

In steps 12 to 15 you create another practice file, without using line numbers.

12. Initiate ED for the PRACTICE.2 file.
13. Create PRACTICE.2 without using line numbering. Use the same text as PRACTICE.1.
14. Terminate ED but don't save the file. Use Q, not Ctrl-C.
15. Check your directory. PRACTICE.2 should not be there.

In steps 16 to 26, practice using the various ED features you studied in this chapter.

16. Initiate ED for PRACTICE.3.
17. Type any nonsense on the ED command line and enter it. You should get a break message.
18. Before continuing make sure echo printing is on, if you have that facility.
19. Initiate insert level.

20.   Type a line that is longer than your console line. Compare the results on your console and your echo printer.

21.   Type a few lines using tabbing to create columns. You could use this data:

```
JAN      FEB      MAR
APR      MAY      JUN
JUL      AUG      SEP
OCT      NOV      DEC
```

22.   Use Ctrl-X to erase your current line.

23.   Terminate insert level.

24.   Abort ED using Ctrl-C.

25.   Check your directory. You should see PRACTICE.3 and PRACTICE.$$$.

26.   Erase PRACTICE.3 and PRACTICE.$$$.

This completes our suggested machine exercise. You may want to spend more time creating some new files and experimenting with ED. When you're ready, shut down your system, and go on to Chapter Nine. Save the PRACTICE.1 file. You'll be using it again later.

Editing Existing Files

In this chapter we discuss how to edit an existing file with ED. You'll learn to code and use many new commands at the ED command level.

When you complete this chapter you will be able to:

- Initiate ED to edit an existing file.
- Move lines from the disk file to memory.
- Display lines on the console.
- Move the character pointer.
- Delete data from memory.
- Insert data in memory.
- Search for and replace data in memory.
- Save the edited data.
- Eliminate the edited data.
- Terminate ED.

STARTING ED

1. To edit an existing file, here's what you'll need available on disk:

        ED.CMD file
            Correct user number or user 0 with system status
        The file to be edited
            Correct user number
        R/W status
            space for ED's $$$ file (at least as much space as the
            existing file)

To initiate the edit, enter ED specific-file-identifier. CP/M-86 will load ED and give it control. ED will then search the indicated disk directory for the file. It also opens the $$$ file.

If the file is found in the directory, ED displays the ED command prompt (*).

(a)   Write the command to edit the file named MAILIST.DOC

    A>____

(b)   Suppose ED.CMD is on disk A and MAILIST.DOC is on disk B. Write the command to edit MAILIST.DOC.

    A>____

(c)   Suppose you have logged on as user 1. ED.CMD is filed under user 1 and MAILIST.DOC is filed under user 3. Can you edit MAILIST.DOC? _______

(d)   Suppose ED.CMD is stored under user 0 with system and R/O status and MAILIST.DOC is stored under user 3 with DIR and R/W status. Under what user number could you edit MAILIST.DOC? _______________________

(e)   Suppose STAT MAILIST.DOC shows that it contains 7K bytes and there are 5K bytes remaining on the disk. Can you edit MAILIST.DOC? _________

—— —— —— —— —— —— ——

(a) A>ED MAILIST.DOC (b) A>ED B:MAILIST.DOC (c) no —the file to be edited must be filed under the current user number; (d) 3; (e) no —there's not enough room for the $$$ file

2.   If all goes well, the opening dialogue should look like this:

```
A>ED MAILIST.DOC
   : *_
```

The file has been found and ED is ready to receive commands.

If ED doesn't find MAILIST.DOC for your user number, the dialogue will look like this:

```
A>ED MAILIST.DOC
NEW FILE
   : *_
```

NEW FILE can be interpreted as a warning message that ED didn't find the file. If you really think that MAILIST.DOC is on the disk, you'll need to get out of ED and resolve the problem. Use Q to quit ED. Then you can use DIR and STAT to find the problem. Was the name misspelled? Is it filed under another user number? Is it on a different disk?

Suppose you want to edit the file named INDEX.DAT. Match the dialogues with their meaning.

_____ (a) `A>ED INDEX.DAT`   1. ED found the file.
            `NEW FILE`   2. ED didn't find the file.
                 `: *_`   3. ED found the file but it has R/O
_____ (b) `A>ED INDEX.DAT`   status.
                `: *_`

In the dialogue below, fill in the commands you would use to get out of ED.

(c) `A>ED INVENTY.DAT`
     `NEW FILE`

      `: *`_____

(d) `Q — (Y/N)?`_____

— — — — — — — — — —

(a) 2; (b) 1; (c) Q (d) Y

3. If your edit file has R/O status you'll get this message:

```
A>ED MAILIST.DOC
** FILE IS READ/ONLY **
    : *_
```

The warning message tells you that you can't make any file changes. However, you can read it under ED if you want. If you really want to change the file, use Q to get out of ED, change the status to R/W, then initiate the edit again.

For the following questions assume that you want to make changes to the existing file named INVENTY.DAT.

Suppose you have this dialogue:

```
A>ED INVENTY.DAT
** FILE IS READ/ONLY **
    : *_
```

(a) What's wrong? ____

____

(b) What command would you enter? *_______

— — — — — — — — — —

(a) the file has R/O status and can't be changed; (b) *Q or *E (you need to quit ED so you can change the status to R/W)

4.   Let's now assume that you have successfully initiated ED and you're ready for the next step.

ED checks for the file but *does not load it*. Your data area in memory is empty. Before you can access, read, or change any file data, you have to load it into memory. You use the A command to do this. A stands for "append."

The format of the A command is: nA. The n indicates the number of lines you want ED to append. If you omit it, ED will append one line; that is, ED will bring one line into memory.

(a)   Show the command to append 5 lines. *_____

(b)   Show the command to append 250 lines. *_____

(c)   Show the command to append 1 line. *_____

(d)   Which of the following best describes the result of the A command?

_____ A.   The indicated number of text lines are moved from memory to disk.

_____ B.   The indicated number of text lines are moved from the disk into memory.

_____ C.   The indicated number of lines are displayed on the console.

— — — — — — — — — — —

(a) 5A (b) 250A (c) A or 1A (d) B

5.   To append all the lines from the file use the command #A. In ED commands # always means 65535. With a long file, this may cause some problems. If ED can't fit the entire file into memory, you'll get this message:

```
        :  *#A
    BREAK  ">"  AT  A
        :  *_
```

ED has loaded as many lines into memory as it could. You can edit those lines, then use the W and A commands to access more lines from the file.

Suppose you have this dialogue:

```
A>ED INVENTY.DAT
     : *#A
BREAK ">" AT A
     : *_
```

What happened?

_____ (a)   ED couldn't find INVENTY.DAT.

_____ (b)   INVENTY.DAT is an empty file.

_____ (c)   ED appended as much of INVENTY.DAT as it could fit in memory.

_____ (d)   INVENTY.DAT wouldn't fit in memory, so ED didn't append anything.

_____ (e)   ED couldn't understand the command.

_____ (f)   ED successfully appended INVENTY.DAT.

— — — — — — — — — —

(c)

6.   A special command is 0A (zero-A). This causes ED to append lines until the memory area is about half-full (or until all lines have been appended, if that happens first.)
What do you suppose the command 0W causes ED to do?

_____ (a)   Write lines until the memory area is about half empty.

_____ (b)   Write lines until the disk file is about half full.

_____ (c)   Write no lines, but empty the memory buffer.

_____ (d)   Write all lines, but don't erase from memory.

— — — — — — — — — —

(a)

ED LINE MANAGEMENT

Before we go any further it's necessary for you to learn how ED manages the various data areas it processes. In the frames that follow we'll show you how ED manages the source file, the temporary file, and the data area in memory.

7. When you enter ED MAILIST.DOC, ED searches the indicated disk directory for MAILIST.DOC. If found, it becomes the *source file*. ED establishes a *source pointer* for the file. The source pointer keeps track of how many lines have been appended from the file.

When you append lines they're copied from the source file, but they're not erased. The source file remains intact throughout the ED function. ED simply moves the source pointer so that it always points to the first "unappended" line.

Suppose MAILIST.DOC contains 100 lines.

(a) If you enter the command *10A, what lines are appended?______________

(b) If you then enter *20A, what lines are appended?______________

(c) If you then enter *#A, what lines are appended?______________

———————————————

(a) lines 1 to 10; (b) lines 11 to 30; (c) lines 31 to 100

8. The diagram below shows the layout of memory when ED is in control. The ED program takes up a portion of memory. The remainder is devoted to storing data lines. We call the data area the *memory buffer*. (In computer terms, a buffer is simply a memory area set aside for storage.)

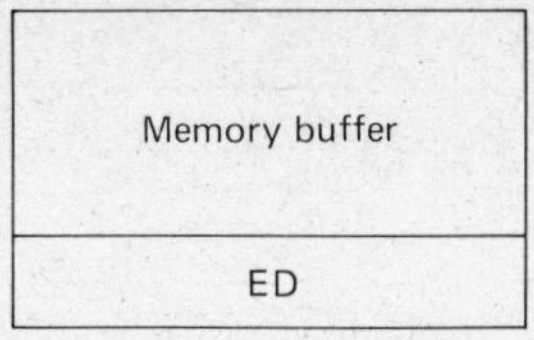

ED maintains a memory pointer that tracks the last line in memory. When you append lines, they're inserted after the memory pointer. Then the memory pointer is moved. The memory pointer keeps newly appended lines from overlaying existing lines in memory.

When you write lines using the W command, they're written from the top line through line n. Then the line numbers for all remaining lines are adjusted, so that line 1 is still the first line in memory. The memory pointer is also moved. It always points to the place where the next line can be appended.

The memory pointer is not the same as the character pointer or the source pointer. The character pointer has a different function, as you'll learn later.

(a)   Select the best definition of "memory buffer."

    _____ A.   All of main memory

    _____ B.   All of memory

    _____ C.   That part of memory that holds data lines

    _____ D.   That part of memory that holds Ed

(b)   Select the best definition of the "memory pointer."

    _____ A.   Always points to the end of the memory buffer

    _____ B.   Always points to the place where the next line can be appended

    _____ C.   Always points to beginning of the memory buffer

— — — — — — — — — —

(a) C; (b) B

9.   When you enter ED MAILIST.DOC, ED opens a new file called MAILIST .$$$. This is called the *temporary file*. When you write lines using the nW command, ED writes them to the $$$ file (or saves them to be written later). A *temporary pointer* keeps track of how many lines are in the file so new lines don't overlay existing ones.

Suppose that the memory buffer currently contains 100 lines and MAILIST.$$$ contains no lines.

(a)   If you enter *10W, which lines are erased from memory? _____________

How many lines are now in MAILIST.$$$?_________________________

(b)   If you then enter *20W, which lines are erased from memory?

____

How many lines are now in MAILIST.$$$? _________________________

— — — — — — — — — —

(a) the first 10, 10; (b) the first 20, 30

10. The three pointers—source, memory, and temporary—keep you from losing, duplicating, or mixing up lines. Lines are moved from the source file, to the memory buffer, to the temporary file in perfect order.

Which of the following statements is true?

_____ (a) You must be careful to always follow an A command with a W command so that appended lines don't get overlaid.

_____ (b) You are free to use any combination of A and W commands; ED will keep track of all lines.

_____ (c) Never use more than one A command and one W command in an edit session or your lines will get mixed up.

— — — — — — — — — —

(b)

Now that you've seen how ED manages all the various sets of lines, let's go back to the edit process.

DISPLAYING LINES

11. Appended lines are not automatically displayed. A typical interaction looks like this:

```
A>ED INVENTY.DAT
  : *#A
 1: *_
```

The lines have been appended and are in memory; you just can't see them. You may find this frustrating at first, but you get used to it after a while.

To display lines, use the T (type) command, which has this format: ±nT. The n gives the number of lines you want typed. The + or − indicates whether you want to go forward from the character pointer (+), or from before it up to the character pointer (−). If you don't specify + or −, + is assumed. If the character pointer is in the middle of a line, T will type that line from the pointer to the end. −T will type that line from the beginning to the pointer.

Suppose memory looks like this:

```
John Jones<CR><LF>16 APPLE WAY<CR><LF>NEW YORK, NY
10010<CR><LF>
```

Match the following commands with their results.

_____ (a) T	1. JOHN JONES
	16 APPLE
_____ (b) +T	2. WAY
	NEW YORK, NY 10010
_____ (c) −T	3. 16 APPLE
_____ (d) 2T	4. WAY
	5. JOHN JONES
_____ (e) −2T	16 APPLE WAY
	NEW YORK, NY 10010
_____ (f) T	
_____ (g) -#T	

————————————

(a) 4; (b) 4; (c) 3; (d) 2; (e) 1; (f) 2; (g) 1

12.   When lines are appended the character pointer is positioned before the first appended line. To type the lines use the nT format. If you use 20T, the first 20 lines in the file will be displayed on the console.

If ED couldn't append all the lines you asked for, the character pointer remains *after* the last line. To see the appended lines, you'll need to use the −nT format. Display at least −2T to get the last line.

The T command does not move the character pointer.

(a)   Suppose you have this dialogue:

```
A>ED INVENTY.DAT
   :   *#A
  1:   *_
```

Show the command to type all the appended lines without moving the

character pointer. *____

(b) Suppose you have this dialogue:

```
A>ED INVENTY.DAT
     :  *#A
BREAK ">" AT A
     :  *_
```

Show the command to display the last appended line without moving the
character pointer. *____

— — — — — — — — — —

(a) *#T; (b) −2T

13. If you type more lines than the screen can hold, the data will roll off the top
of the screen.

You can prevent this by typing one less line than your screen can hold. For
example, the monochrome display shows 24 lines so we ordinarily use the
command 23T. The 24th line is needed for ED to display the command prompt
after the T command has been processed.

If the data lines take more than one screen line each, we need to adjust the type
command accordingly. Therefore if we want to type records that take two
console lines each, we use the command 11T.

If we're just scanning the file, we'll let it roll off the top. We can use the Ctrl-S
function to interupt the display and any other character to abort the command.
We can use Ctrl-P to cause echo printing, which slows down the screen display.

Suppose your video screen has 20 lines.

(a) What command would you use to view a screenful of lines? *__________

(b) What command would you use if the text lines each take three screen lines?

   *_____

(c) What command would you use to scan the entire file? *______________

(d) How could you interrupt the display?______________________________

(e) Once the display has been interrupted how can you restart the display?

   ____

(f) How can you abort the command? *________________________________

— — — — — — — — — —

(a) *19T; (b) *6T; (c) *#T or any large n such as *999T; (d) type Ctrl-S; (e) type
any character except Ctrl-C; (f) Ctrl-C

14. Write the commands to edit the short MAILIST.DOC file, append all the lines, and display all the appended lines.

(a) A>____

(b)   : *______

(c)   1: *______

(d) Where is the character pointer now?

______ A. at the beginning of the file

______ B. at the end of the file

______ C. somewhere in the middle of the file

— — — — — — — — — —

(a) A>ED MAILIST.DOC (b) *#A (c) *#T (d) A

CHARACTER POINTER COMMANDS

In the following frames we'll show you the commands to move the character pointer.

15. To move the pointer a specific number of characters, use the C (characters) command which has this format: ±nC.

(a) Write the command to move the character pointer forward five characters.

*______

(b) Write the command to move the character pointer backward 10 characters.

*______

(c) Write the command to move the character pointer forward one character.

*______

(d) Write the command to move the character pointer backward one character.

*______

(e) Write the command to move the character pointer forward 65535 characters.

*______

(f) Write the command to move the character pointer backward 65535 characters.

*______

—————————

(a) *5C or *+5C (b) *–10C (c) *C or *+C or *1C or *+1C (d) *–C or *–1C (e) *#C or *+#C (f) *–#C (You could also use 65535 in place of #)

16.   To move the character pointer a specific number of lines, use the L (lines) command, which has this format: ±nL.

If the character pointer is in the middle of a line, it is first moved to the beginning of the line, then moved the indicated number of lines. After an L command the character pointer is always positioned at the beginning of a line (or at the end of the data in memory). *L or *+L means *+1L; the character pointer is moved to the beginning of the current line, if necessary, then moved forward one line. *–L means *–1L; the character pointer is moved to the beginning of the current line, if necessary, then moved one line towards the beginning of the file. A special command, *0L (zero-L), moves the character pointer to the beginning of the current line.

Suppose memory looks like this:

ABC<CR><LF>DEF<CR><LF>GHI

Match the following commands with their results.

_____ (a) L

_____ (b) +L

_____ (c) –L

_____ (d) +2L

_____ (e) –2L

_____ (f) 0L

1.   ^ABC<CR><LF>DEF<CR><LF>GHI
2.   ABC<CR><LF>DEF<CR><LF>GHI
3.   ABC<CR><LF>DEF<CR><LF>GHI
4.   ABC<CR><LF>DEF<CR><LF>GHI
5.   ABC<CR><LF>DEF<CR><LF>GHI ^

—————————

(a) 4; (b) 4; (c) 1; (d) 5; (e) 1; (f) 2

17.   To move the character pointer to the beginning or end of the data lines in memory, use the B (beginning or bottom) command, which has this format: ±B. B or +B refers to the beginning of the file, and –B refers to the end. (This is the only command where – refers to a position nearer the end than the beginning.)

Match the B commands with their equivalent C and L commands.

_____ (a) B		1.	+#C
_____ (b) −B		2.	#C
		3.	−#C
		4.	−C
		5.	+L
		6.	#L
		7.	−#L

— — — — — — — — — —

(a) 3, 7; (b) 1, 2, 6

18. If line numbering is on you can also move the character pointer to the beginning of a specified line. You do this by typing the line number followed by a colon at the ED prompt, like this:

    *5:

You can put the line number in front of another ED command. For example, to type line 5 you would enter 5:T. To type 10 lines, starting with line 5, you would enter 5:10T. To type 3 lines ending with 5, you would enter: 5:−3T. Lines 2, 3, and 4 would then be typed (up to the character pointer).

(a) Show the command to move the character pointer to the beginning of line 100. *_____

(b) Show the command to move the character pointer to the beginning of line 40 and type that line. *_____

(c) Show the command to move the character pointer to the beginning of line 10 and type lines 1 to 9. *_____

(d) Show the command to move the character pointer to the beginning of line 1 and type all lines. *_____

— — — — — — — — — —

(a) *100: (b) *40:T or *40:1T or *40:+1T (c) *10:−#T or *10:−9T (d) *1:#T or *1:+#T

From now on we won't show you all the possible variations of a correct answer. We'll show you the preferred format, which is usually the shortest, as in *40:T above.

19. You can also specify that a command be executed *through* a line number. To do this, put the colon before the line number. For example, :10T means to type from the character pointer through line 10. The character pointer is not moved. Note that when you use this command format you can't also specify the number of lines. The command :10+5T makes no sense. You can, however, combine a beginning and ending line reference. The command 2::10T would move the character pointer to the beginning of line 2 and type lines 2 through 10. The character pointer would remain at the beginning of line 2.

Write the appropriate commands for the following functions:

(a) Type from the character pointer through line 100. *_____

(b) Move the character pointer to line 100 and type through line 120.

  *_____

— — — — — — — — — — —

(a) *:100T (b) 100::120T

20. You can use a special (and very convenient) abbreviation to move the pointer a specific number of lines and type the new current line. Simply enter ±n. For example, the command *5 means to move forward five lines and type. *–3 means to move backward three lines and type.

If you simply press Enter, ED will interpret it as +1 and move down 1 line and type it.

Suppose memory contains these lines:

```
1:   THIS IS LINE 1
2:   THIS IS LINE 2
3:   THIS IS LINE 3
4:   THIS IS LINE 4
5:   THIS IS LINE 5
```

Starting from line 1, state what line will be typed by each of the following commands.

(a) Enter ____

(b) *2 ____

(c) Enter ____

(d) *–3 ____

(e) Enter ____

— — — — — — — — — —

(a) 2; (b) 4; (c) 5; (d) 2; (e) 3

21. As long as the character pointer is within the stored data lines, the displayed line number shows which line contains the character pointer. It isn't necessarily at the beginning of that line, but it's somewhere in the indicated line. You should be able to tell where, by what happened previously.

(a) Suppose your display looks like this:

```
A>ED OLDFILE
    : *#A
  1: *_
```

Where is the character pointer? _______________________________________

(b) Continuing the above example:

```
1: *3T
1:   THIS IS LINE 1
2:   THIS IS LINE 2
3:   THIS IS LINE 3
1: *_
```

Where is the character pointer now? _______________________________________

(c) Continuing the above example:

```
1: *3
4:   THIS IS LINE 4
4: *_
```

Where is the character pointer now? _______________________________________

(d) Continuing the above example:

```
4: *-2L
2: *_
```

Where is the character pointer now? _______________________________________

(e) Continuing the above example:

```
    2: *5C
    2: *T
IS LINE 2
    2: *_
```

Where is the character pointer now? _______________________________________

— — — — — — — — — —

(a) beginning of line 1; (b) still at the beginning of line 1; (c) beginning of line 4; (d) beginning of line 2; (e) middle of line 2

DELETE COMMANDS

Now that you've learned how to move the character pointer and type lines, we'll show you how to delete data from memory.

22. To delete one or more characters from memory, use the D (delete) command. Its format is ±nD. It deletes n characters forward or backward from the character pointer. The character pointer is not moved.
  Suppose your memory looks like this:

ABC<CR><LF>DEF<CR><LF>GHI

Match the commands with their results. (Apply each to the memory contents above.)

_____ (a) *#D

_____ (b) *2D

_____ (c) *–1D

_____ (d) *D

_____ (e) *–#D

_____ (f) *–4D

_____ (g) *1D

_____ (h) *–D

1. ABC<CR><LF>DF<CR><LF>GHI
2. ABC<CR><LF>DE<CR><LF>GHI
3. F<CR><LF>GHI
4. ABC<CR><LF>DE
5. ABCF<CR><LF>GHI
6. ABC<CR><LF>DEGHI
7. ABC<CR><LF>DE<LF>GHI

____

(a) 4; (b) 7; (c) 1; (d) 2; (e) 3; (f) 5; (g) 2; (h) 1

23. You can see that the position of the character pointer is very important when you're using the delete commands. Don't forget that you can always find out where the character pointer is by using the T command. You can move it by using the C, L, or B commands, or absolute line references. It's also extremely important to remember that T *does not move* the character pointer.

Suppose your display currently looks like this:

```
  :  *B
1:  *3T
1:    JOHN JONES
2:    16 APPLE ST.
3:    NEW YORK, NY 10010
1:  *_
```

(a) Where is the character pointer? ___________________________________

(b) Suppose you want to delete the characters "ST." Write the command, or

commands, to move the character pointer so it precedes the S. *________

(c) Write the command to display the new position of the character pointer.

*_____

(d) What display would you expect from the command you wrote in (c)?

____

(e) Assuming that the character pointer now precedes "ST. ," write the com-

mand to delete these characters. *___________________________________

(f) Write the command to confirm that the characters were correctly deleted.

*_____

— — — — — — — — — — —

(a) at the beginning of the first line; (b) there are several ways to do this. You could use *21C (remembering to count <CR> and <LF>), or you could use *L followed by *9C, or *2L followed by *−5C, or you could use an absolute line reference as in 2:9C or 3:−5C; (c) *T (d) ST. ; (e) *3D (f) *2:T would be the best choice as it would display all of line 2; *T would show whether there was anything between the character pointer and the end of the line; *−T would not do as it would only display up to the character pointer.

24. To delete entire lines, use the K (kill) command which has this format: ±K. +K kills up *through* the next <CR><LF>. –K kills through the preceding <CR><LF>, all the way to the next <CR><LF>.

The following diagram depicts the range of +K and –K.

$$-K \qquad\qquad +K$$

ABC<CR><LF>DEF<CR><LF>GHI<CR><LF>

Suppose your display looks like this:

```
1: *B
1: *8T
1: JOHN JONES
2: 16 APPLE
3: NEW YORK, NY 10010
4:
5: MARY SMITH
6: 10 FIELDING CT.
7: PITTSBURGH, PA 15213
8:
1: *_
```

Which of the following commands could be used to kill lines 5–8?

______ (a)   *–3K

______ (b)   *5:4K

______ (c)   *5::8K

______ (d)   *8K

______ (e)   *:8K

______ (f)   *4L followed by *4K

______ (g)   –4L followed by *4K

— — — — — — — — — — —

(b), (c), and (f) [(a) would kill nothing; (d) and (e) would kill lines 1 to 8; (g) would kill lines 1 to 4]

25. If the character pointer is in the middle of a line, K will kill from the character pointer through the end of the line. –K will kill from the beginning of the preceding line up to the character pointer. Refer to the diagram in frame 24 again and you'll see why.

Suppose your memory looks like this:

ABC<CR><LF>DEF<CR><LF>GHI

Match the delete commands with their effect.

_____ (a) *K

_____ (b) *–K

_____ (c) *2K

_____ (d) *–2K

1. ABC<CR><LF>GHI
2. ABC<CR><LF>DEGHI
3. ABC<CR><LF>
4. F<CR><LF>GHI
5. ABCF<CR><LF>GHI
6. ABC<CR><LF>DE

– – – – – – – – – –

(a) 2; (b) 4; (c) 6; (d) 4

26. Line numbering under ED is dynamic. As you kill lines the remaining lines are renumbered instantaneously. You won't see the line numbers change however, unless you redisplay the text after every kill command. Therefore when you're using absolute line references in your commands, you'll want to be careful that the numbers don't change.

Suppose your display currently looks like this:

```
7:  *B
1:  *8T
1:  JOHN JONES
2:  16 APPLE
3:  NEW YORK, NY 10010
4:
5:  MARY SMITH
6:  10 FIELDING CT.
7:  PITTSBURGH, PA 15213
8:
1:  *_
```

(a)   Suppose you enter these commands:

>   1: *3:K
>   3: *4:T

What line will be displayed?

_______ 4:   NEW YORK, NY 10010

_______ 4:

_______ 4:   MARY SMITH

(b)   Go back to the original display and write the commands to kill lines 2 and 6. Use absolute line references.

*____

*____

— — — — — — — — — — —

(a) MARY SMITH; (b) *2:K *5:K

INSERT COMMAND

When you're editing an existing file you may want to insert new data. In the following frames we'll show you how to do that.

27.   To insert data in memory, use the I (or i) command. I will insert the data immediately before the character pointer. You can either go into insert level, as you learned before, or include the insert data directly in the I command.

To enter the insert level, type I followed by the Enter key. ED gets ready to receive new data but does not start a new line. The data you type next will be inserted before the character pointer, wherever that is.

Let's examine three cases.

In case number 1 we want to insert an apartment number in John Jones' address. First we confirm the first three lines. Then we use Enter to move down and confirm the second line. We then invoke insert level and type "APT. #101". We follow it with <CR> because we want it to be a separate line, and then we use Ctrl-Z to end insert level. Finally, we confirm our work.

```
1:  *3T
1:   JOHN JONES
2:   16 APPLE RD.
3:   NEW YORK, NY 10010
1:  *<CR>
2:   16 APPLE RD.
2:  *I
2:   APT. #101<CR>
3:   ^Z
3:   1::4T
1:   JOHN JONES
2:   APT. #101
3:   16 APPLE RD.
4:   NEW YORK, NY 10010
1:  *_
```

In the second case, we want to change MARY SMITH to read MARY ANN SMITH. First we get the character pointer to the desired position, between the space and the S. Then we invoke insert level. We type ANN, a space, and Ctrl-Z. The four characters are inserted before the character pointer. The character pointer is still in the middle of the line so we have to use 6:T to see the whole line.

```
6:  *T
6:   MARY SMITH
6:  *5C
6:  *I
6:   ANN ^Z
6:  *6:T
6:   MARY ANN SMITH
6:  *
```

In our last case we want to put the zip code on a separate line. So we want to insert <CR><LF> in between NY and 10010. First we position the character pointer. Then we enter insert level and insert <CR>. ED will automatically supply the <LF>. The <CR><LF> puts us at the beginning of line 5, where we end the insert. Then we go back to line 4 and type two lines to confirm our work.

```
4:  *T
4:   NEW YORK, NY 10010
4:  *13C
4:  *I
4:   <CR>
5:   ^Z
5:  *4:2T
4:   NEW YORK, NY
5:   10010
4:  *_
```

(a) Suppose you have this display:

```
1:  *4T
1:   THIS IS LINE 1
2:   THIS IS LINE
3:   THIS IS LINE 3
4:   THIS IS LINE 4
1:  *_
```

You want to correct the second line so that it reads THIS IS LINE 2. Show the commands to do this. (You'll need to insert a space before the 2.)

____

____

____

____

____

____

____

____

____

(b) Suppose you have this display:

```
1:  *4T
1:   MEMO TO ALL STAFF
2:   RE:  LOCKUP PROCEDURES
3:
4:   IT HAS BEEN BROUGHT TO MY ATTENTION
1:  *_
```

You want to insert a new second line that reads FROM THE SECURITY OFFICER. Show the commands to do this.

____

____

____

____

____

____

____

____

————————————

There are many correct solutions to these two problems. We can't show them all; so we'll show a suggested answer to each one.

```
(a)  1:  *<CR>
     2:   THIS IS LINE
     2:  *12C
     2:  *-T
     2:  *THIS IS LINE
     2:  *I
     2:   2^Z
     2:  *2:T<CR>
     2:  *_

(b)  1:  *2:I
     2:   FROM THE SECURITY OFFICER <CR> CR
     3:   ^Z
     3:  *1:3T
     1:   MEMO TO ALL STAFF
     2:   FROM THE SECURITY OFFICER
     3:   RE:   LOCKUP PROCEDURES
     1:  *_
```

28.   You don't have to enter insert level to insert data. You can type the insert data immediately after the I command. There are two ways to terminate the insert. You can use Ctrl-Z or <CR>. <CR> will terminate the command and cause <CR><LF> to be inserted at the end of the new data. Ctrl-Z will simply terminate the command with no <CR><LF>.

We'll redo the three cases from the previous frame, this time without using insert level.

To insert the apartment line in John Jones' address, we first position the character pointer at the beginning of line 2. We then type the command IAPT. #101 and terminate it with <CR>. Notice that this puts us on line 3. Then we type four lines to confirm our work.

```
1:  *3T
1:   JOHN JONES
2:   16 APPLE RD.
3:   NEW YORK, NY 10010
1:  *<CR>
2:   16 APPLE RD
2:  *IAPT. #101<CR>
3:  *1:4T
1:   JOHN JONES
2:   APT. #101
1:   16 APPLE RD.
4:   NEW YORK, NY 10010
1:  *_
```

To change MARY SMITH to MARY ANN SMITH, we first position the character pointer. We then type the command IANN ^Z. Notice that we include a space in the command so that ANN doesn't run into SMITH. Since we terminated with Ctrl-Z, no <CR><LF> is inserted.

```
6:  *T
6:    MARY SMITH
6:  *5C
6:  *IANN ^Z
6:  *6:T
6:    MARY ANN SMITH
6:  *_
```

To make the zip code into a new line we first position the character pointer. Then we type the command I   <CR>. We have to put a space in the command, or ED will put us in insert level! The space will be inserted on line 4, but it should not do any damage there. The <CR> terminates the command and inserts <CR><LF> before the 10010, putting the zip code on line 5. Don't forget that the remaining lines will be renumbered immediately.

```
4:  *T
4:    NEW YORK, NY 10010
4:  *13C
4:    I <CR>
5:    4:2T
4:    NEW YORK, NY
5:    10010
```

Answer the questions in frame 27 again. This time don't use insert level.

(a) Suppose you have this display:

```
1:  *4T
1:    THIS IS LINE 1
2:    THIS IS LINE
3:    THIS IS LINE 3
4:    THIS IS LINE 4
1:  *_
```

You want to correct the second line so that it reads THIS IS LINE 2. Show the commands to do this. (You'll need to insert a space before the 2.)

____

____

____

____

____

____

____

____

____

(b) Suppose you have this display:

```
1: *4T
1:    MEMO TO ALL STAFF
2:    RE: LOCKUP PROCEDURES
3:
4:    IT HAS BEEN BROUGHT TO MY ATTENTION
1: *_
```

You want to insert a new second line that reads FROM THE SECURITY OFFICER. Show the commands to do this.

____

____

____

____

____

____

____

— — — — — — — — — — —

Suggested answers:

(a)
```
1: *<CR>
2:    THIS IS LINE
2: *12C
2: *-T
2:    THIS IS LINE
2: *I 2^Z
2: *2:T
2:    THIS IS LINE 2
2: *_
```

(b)
```
1: *2:IFROM THE SECURITY OFFICER<CR>
2: *1:3T
1:    MEMO TO ALL STAFF
2:    FROM THE SECURITY OFFICER
3:    RE: LOCKUP PROCEDURES
1: *_
```

SEARCH AND REPLACE COMMANDS

By combining character pointer commands, delete commands, and insert commands, you can change a file in any way. But some types of changes would be quite tedious. For example, try going through a 1000 line report and changing all occurrences of 1989 to 1990. ED provides search and replace commands to make this task easier.

29.   You can ask ED to search memory for a specified string of characters. The format of the command is Fstring. (F is for "find.") For example, if you want to find the word JONES you would enter FJONES or fJONES. ED will start at the character pointer and search forward until the five letters (JONES) are found. ED moves the character pointer to the position *after* the last character of the matching string. You can then enter an insert or delete command, or whatever is appropriate to your task.

The F command is a faster way of moving the character pointer. If your file contains both upper- and lowercase letters, you must use a lowercase f, and the search string must match the found string exactly. For example, FJones will find "JONES". If you specify fJones, ED will find "Jones" but not "JONES" or "jones". If you use an uppercase search command, you'll find uppercase characters. If you use a lowercase search command, you can specify exactly how the string appears. Numbers can be located either way.

(a)   Write a command to search for the next occurrence of "ABCdef."

*_____

(b)   Where does the search start? ____

(c)   In what direction does the search go: forward, backward, or both? ______

(d)   How does ED mark a matching string?

_____ A.   By displaying the line

_____ B.   By displaying the line number

_____ C.   By putting the character pointer before the string

_____ D.   By putting the character pointer after the string

_ _ _ _ _ _ _ _ _ _

(a) *fABCdef; (b) at the character pointer, (c) forward; (d) D

30. Be very careful of the search strings you enter. You may get a match you didn't expect. For example, suppose memory looks like this:

```
MEMO TO ALL STAFF<CR><LF>RE: STAXNDING
ORDERS<CR><LF>
```

You want to delete the typo in "STAXNDING" so you enter FSTA. What will happen?

```
MEMO TO ALL STAFF<CR><LF>RE: STAXNDING
ORDERS<CR><LF>
```

ED found the next occurrence of the string "STA." Your display would look like this:

```
1: *FSTA
1: *_
```

You wouldn't necessarily know that ED found the wrong string unless you notice that you're on line 1. It's wise to always use T after F to see exactly what ED found.

Suppose your display looks like this:

```
1: *5T
1:   JOHN JONES
2:   APT. #101
3:   16 APPLE RD.
4:   NEW YORK, NY
5:   10010
1: *_
```

It turns out that Mr. Jones' zip code is 10920. You want to find the zip code, delete 01, and insert 92.

(a)   Which of the following search commands is better?

______   F10

______   F100

______   F1001

______   F10010

(b)   Why? ____

____

____

— — — — — — — — — — —

(a) F1001 or f1001; (b) F10 would find the apartment number 101. F100 would find the zip code 100, but the character pointer would be in an awkward place to delete 01 and insert 92. F1001 would find 10010 and leave the character pointer in good position for *–2D followed by *I92. F10010 would also work, but you'd have to use *–3D followed by *I920.

31.   The F command can be preceded by a number. For example, 3FJONES would find the *third* occurrence of JONES. The first two occurrences would be found and then bypassed.

(a)   Write a command to find the second occurrence of the string "10".

*____

(b)   Write a command to find the fourth occurrence of the string

"Ashley". *____

— — — — — — — — — — —

(a) *2F10 (b) *4fAshley

32. Now let's go back and redo the first problem from frame 27. This time use the F command to position the character pointer.
Suppose you have this display:

```
1:  *4T
1:    THIS IS LINE 1
2:    THIS IS LINE
3:    THIS IS LINE 3
4:    THIS IS LINE 4
1:  *_
```

You want to correct the second line so that it reads THIS IS LINE 2. Show the commands to do this. (You'll need to insert a space before the 2.)

____

____

____

____

____

____

____

____

____

____

— — — — — — — — — —

Suggested answer:

```
1: *2FLINE
2: *-T
2:   THIS IS LINE
2: *I 2^Z
2: *-T
2:   THIS IS LINE 2
2: *_
```

(you could use lowercase f if you prefer)

33.   If ED gets to the memory pointer without finding a match, you'll get this message: BREAK "#" AT. The character pointer remains in its original position.
Suppose you have this display:

```
7:  *B
1:  *FMAX
1:   BREAK "#" AT
1:  *_
```

(a)   What happened? ____

____

(b)   Where is the character pointer now? ___________________________

____

— — — — — — — — — —

(a) ED couldn't find "MAX"; (b) at the beginning of memory

34.   If your file is larger than the memory buffer, you can search the whole file using the N command. An uppercase or lowercase letter can be used with the same effect as with the F command. N combines F, W, and A commands in this fashion:

1.   Text data in memory is searched. If a match is found, the command terminates normally as with F.
2.   If a match is not found, all lines in memory are written to the temporary file. This is equivalent to a #W command.
3.   Lines are then appended from the source file until memory is about half full or the source file is exhausted. This is equivalent to a 0A command.
4.   Steps 1 through 3 are repeated until a match is found or the source file is exhausted.

Use this command wisely. Once lines to the temporary file have been written, you can't retrieve them again without ending the edit and starting over.
Write a command to search the entire MAILIST.DOC file for ART DECO, LTD.

```
A>ED MAILIST.DOC
```

: *____

— — — — — — — — — —

*NART DECO, LTD. or *nART DECO, LTD.

35. Sometimes you need to search for a string containing <CR><LF>, but you can't type <CR> or the command will be entered and processed. Use Ctrl-L as a substitute for <CR><LF>. When ED reads Ctrl-L it searches for <CR><LF>.

Write a command to search for NY<CR><LF>10010. *_______________

— — — — — — — — — —

*FNY^L10010 or *fNY^L10010 (^L is Ctrl-L)

Now that you've learned how to search for strings, we'll show you how to replace them.

36. Replacement is a combined process of deleting old characters and inserting new ones. You can do this with one ED command, the S (substitute) command. S combines searching, deleting, and inserting. The format is

      nSold-string^Znew-string

You can use uppercase or lowercase S with the same effects as in the N or F command. If no n is given, ED will search for the next occurrence of old-string and replace it with new-string. If n is given, it indicates how many strings should be replaced. This is different from the F command, which says to find the nth string. The character pointer is positioned after the last character of the replacement.

The number of characters in old-string and new-string do not need to be the same.

(a) Write a command to find *all* occurrences of JONES and replace with JOHN-

SON. *____

(b) Can you use the S command to search for and replace only the fourth

occurrence of Jones with Johnson? ____ If so, show the command.

*____

— — — — — — — — — —

(a) *#SJONES^ZJOHNSON (b) no—*4sJONES^ZJOHNSON would replace the next four occurrences

37.   The S command can be used to great advantage in some applications. For example, suppose you want to send a personalized letter to ten potential clients. You can set the text of the letter up so that an * indicates the receiver's name thus:

```
Dear *,
I enjoyed talking to you at yesterday's NSPI meeting. I
indicated that I had a short—term investment program
that you may be interested in. I've been reviewing the
information you gave me, *, and I'm sure that this plan is
perfect for you. Etc. Etc.
```

Write the command to replace all occurrences of * in this file with Bob.

*____

— — — — — — — — — — —

#s^ZBob (be sure you used a lowercase s)

38.   One final search and replace command gives you even more flexibility in changing a text. This is the J (juxtaposition) command.

J involves three strings: a search string, an insert string, and a termination string. This is how it works. ED searches memory for the search string. The insert string is inserted *after* the search string in memory. The two strings are placed next to each other, or juxtaposed. Finally, all characters following the insert are deleted up to the termination string.

Confusing? An example will help. Suppose we want to change all JONES to JOHNSON. We'll make JO the search string. The insert string is HNSON. The termination string is a space. Now watch what happens.

First, Ed locates JO.   MR. JONES
Then ED inserts HNSON.   MR. JOHNSONNES
Finally, ED deletes up to the next space.   MR. JOHNSON

The format of the J command is nJsearch-string^Zinsert-string^Ztermination-string. As with the other search commands, an upper or lower case letter can be used. In the above JONES-to-JOHNSON example, the command would be #JJO^ZHSON^Z   <CR>.

(a)   Write a command to change all occurrences of "DUOTECH" to

     "DUOTECH, INC." *_______________________________________

(b)   Write a command to change all occurrences of "DuoTech" to

     "DuoTech, Inc." *_______________________________________

————————

(a) *#JDUOTECH^Z, INC.^Z, <CR> (b) *#jDuoTech^Z, Inc.^Z <CR>

39. You have now learned the search and replace commands.

- F finds one matching string and moves the character pointer, but takes no other action.
- N is like F but will search the entire file, not just what's in memory.
- S finds a matching string and substitutes another string for it.
- J finds a matching string, juxtaposes an insert string, and deletes characters up to a termination string.

If any string needs to include <CR><LF>, use Ctrl-L in the command. Ed interprets Ctrl-L as <CR><LF>.

(a) Write a command to find the next occurrence of "PROJECT STAR".

   *____

(b) Write a command to move the character pointer to line 10 and find the third

   occurrence of the letter "X". *_______________________________________

(c) Write a command to replace the next five occurrences of "COMPUTER"

   with "SYSTEM". *____

(d) Change the above command so that the "COMPUTER" is changed only if it's a separate word. That is, change "OUR COMPUTER IS" to "OUR SYSTEM IS" but don't change "THE MICROCOMPUTER" or "COMPUTER

   ASSISTED INSTRUCTION". *____

(e) Write a command to go to line 3, find the phrase "COST FACTOR" and split the line beteen "COST" and "FACTOR". Delete the space between the two words so that one line ends with "COST<CR><LF>" and the next line

   starts with "FACTOR". *____

(f) Now write a command to delete the <CR><LF> after "FACTOR" on line 4. (Assume that the character pointer is positioned at the beginning of line 4.)

   *____

————————

(a) *FPROJECT STAR or *NPROJECT STAR (b) *10:3FX (c) *5SCOMPUTER^ZSYSTEM (d) *5S COMPUTER ^Z SYSTEM <CR> [We included the terminating <CR> to show that a space precedes it; note that this command would not change "COMPUTER." at the end of a sentence.]; (e) 3:JCOST^Z^L^ZF (f) S^L^Z <CR> [Did you think to insert a space after ^Z? Otherwise "FACTOR" will run into the next word with no intervening space.]

————————

TERMINATING ED

Let's assume now that you've made all the changes you want to the old file. In the frames that follow we'll review how to get out of ED and back to CCP level.

40.   Let's review the condition of the disk files and memory after you've made some editing changes.

The source file is still on the disk. You've moved lines from this file into memory and have changed them, but no changes have been made to the original disk file itself; it's still intact, and it still has the same name. The source pointer shows the number of lines that have already been appended to memory from this file.

A temporary file called filename.$$$ also exists on the disk. If you have not written any lines, it is empty. However, if you've used the W command, the file would contain some edited lines. The N command may also have written some lines to the $$$ file. The temporary pointer shows how many lines this file currently contains.

Suppose you've been editing INVENTY.DOC. Match the data areas with their contents.

____ (a)   INVENTY.DOC

____ (b)   INVENTY.$$$

____ (c)   Memory buffer

1.   Edited lines
2.   Unchanged source lines

_ _ _ _ _ _ _ _ _ _ _

(a) 2; (b) 1; (c) 1

41.   Let's assume now that you want to take a normal exit from ED. That is, you want to save the editing work that you've done. The command is E, for exit.

In response to the E command, ED does the following:

1.   Writes all lines from main memory to the $$$ file. (Equivalent to #W.)
2.   Transfers any unused lines from the source file to the $$$ file. (Equivalent to repeating #A followed by #W until the source file is empty.) Note that the $$$ file now contains a complete, edited file.
3.   Renames the source file as filename.BAK. This file will stay on the disk so you can get back to your original version if you wish. If the disk already contains a filename.BAK, the earlier version is erased.
4.   Renames the $$$ file with the original file identifier. If you edited MAILIST.DOC, then the source file becomes MAILIST.BAK and the "temporary" file becomes MAILIST.DOC.
5.   Returns control to the CCP.

Suppose you edit a file named INVENTY.DOC. You make several changes, then terminate the edit with E.

(a) What files would you expect to see on the disk directory?

   ____ A. INVENTY.DOC

   ____ B. INVENTY.$$$

   ____ C. INVENTY.BAK

   ____ D. $$$.BAK

   ____ E. INVENTY.2

(b) Which of the above files would contain the new version of INVENTY.DOC?

____

(c) Which of the above files would contain the old version of INVENTY.DOC?

____

(Extra thought questions) Suppose you want to make some more editing changes to INVENTY.DOC. You enter ED INVENTY.DOC, make the changes, and enter E.

(d) Where is the *third* version of INVENTY.DOC? _______________________

(e) Where is the *second* version of INVENTY.DOC? _______________________

(f) Where is the *original* (or first) version of INVENTY.DOC? _______________

(g) Suppose you want to create and keep five versions of the INVENTY file on the same disk. After you create the second version, what should you do before you enter ED INVENTY.DOC again?

____

____

(h) You should never try to edit a BAK file. Why?

____

____

____

____

____

(a) A and C; (b) INVENTY.DOC; (c) INVENTY.BAK; (d) in INVENTY.DOC; (e) in INVENTY.BAK; (f) erased and gone forever; (g) rename INVENTY.BAK as INVENTY.V1 or INVENTY.ORG or some other name so that it doesn't get erased; (h) when the E command is processed, ED erases any existing filename.BAK. Your original file will be erased. ED will then attempt to rename filename.BAK (the original file, which just got erased) as filename.BAK. This command will fail, because there is no file to be renamed

42.   Suppose you want to get out of Ed without saving your editing changes. The command is Q. ED will do the following.

1.   Confirm that you mean to quit.
2.   Erase the $$$ file.
3.   Leave the original file alone.
4.   Return control to the CCP.

Suppose you enter ED INVENTY.DOC. You then append some lines, make some changes, write some lines, append more lines, and make more changes. Then you enter the Q command.

(a)   What files would you expect to find on the disk directory?

_____ A.   INVENTY.DOC

_____ B.   INVENTY.BAK

_____ C.   INVENTY.$$$

(b)   Which of the above files, if any, contains your original version of INVENTY.DOC? ____

(c)   Which of the above files, if any, contains the lines that you wrote while editing? ____

Suppose you used Ctrl-C to terminate ED instead of the Q command.

(d)   What files would you expect to find on the disk directory?

_____ A.   INVENTY.DOC

_____ B.   INVENTY.BAK

_____ C.   INVENTY.$$$

(e)   Which of the above files, if any, contains your original version of INVENTY.DOC? ____

(f)   Which of the above files, if any, contains the lines that you wrote while editing? ____

- - - - - - - - - - -

(a) A; (b) INVENTY.DOC; (c) none; (d) A and C; (e) INVENTY.DOC; (f) INVENTY.$$$

43. Don't forget about the H and O commands we mentioned in Chapter Eight. The O (original) command eliminates your editing work and lets you start over. When you enter O, ED does the following:

1. Confirms that you want to return to the source file.
2. Erases the $$$ file.
3. Moves the source pointer to the beginning of the source file again.
4. Opens a new $$$ file.
5. Returns the ED command prompt.

The H (head) command saves your editing work and lets you start doing some more editing. When you enter H, ED does the following:

1. Finalizes the $$$ file—transfers all remaining lines from memory and from the source file.
2. Erases any existing filename.BAK.
3. Renames the source file as filename.BAK.
4. Renames the $$$ file as filename.typ.
5. Opens the newly named filename.typ file as the source file.
6. Opens a new $$$ file.
7. Returns the ED command prompt.

(a) Which command is equivalent to *E followed by A>ED filename? _____

(b) Which command is equivalent to *Q followed by A>ED filename? _____

(c) Which command will cause you to eventually lose your original source file if you later take a normal exit from ED? _____

(d) With which command will you need to append more lines to continue editing? _____

(Extra thought question)

(e) Suppose you used an N command and most of your lines got written out to the $$$ file. But you want to do more editing on the lines that were written. You can't append them because the A command reads lines from the source file, not the $$$ file. What can you do? _________________________

_ _ _ _ _ _ _ _ _ _

(a) H; (b) O; (c) H; (d) H and O; (e) use H to restart ED using the new file

Now you've seen how to edit an existing file using ED. You've learned how to initiate the edit, append lines, move the character pointer around, display lines, delete characters or lines, insert data, find data, replace data, juxtapose data, and end the edit session. The Self-Test will give you a chance to review and practice the material you've studied. You'll then get a chance to actually try your hand at changing the file you created before.

Chapter Nine Self-Test

For this Self-Test, we'll go through the corrections to the file shown in Figure 9.1. The typed material shows the SECURITY.MEM file as it currently exists. The handwritten material shows the desired corrections.

```
                     SENIOR
 1:    MEMO TO ALL STAFF

 2:    FROM THE SECURITY OFFICER
              NIGHTLY
 3:    RE: LOCKUP PROCEDURES

 4:    DATE: 5/14/82
                   CALLED
 5:    IT HAS BEEN BROUGHT TO MY ATTENTION THAT STAFF

 6:    MEMBERS HAVE NOT BEEN PROPERLY SECURING THE

 7:    BUILDING AT NIGHT.  THE LAST PERSON TO LEAVE

 8:    THE BUILDING MUST FOLLOW THESE PROCEDURES:

 9:

10:        1.  ENSURE THAT ALL WINDOWS ARE LOCKED.

11:

12:        2.  UNPLUG THE COFFEE POT.

13:

14:        3.  TURN OFF ALL LIGHTS. EXCEPT THE

15:           CENTRAL HALL.

16:        4. TURN OFF THE OUTSIDE LIGHTS.
                         DOOR
17:        5. BOLT THE BACK EXIT FROM THE INSIDE.

18:

19:
                            DOOR
20:        6. LEAVE BY FRONT EXIT.

21:
                              DOOR
22:        7. USE KEY TO LOCK FRONT EXIT.

23:

24:    VIOLATIONS WILL BE PUNISHED.

25:                        E. J. LOCKWOOD
```

Figure 9.1 SECURITY.MEM File

1. Write the command to initiate the edit.

   A>____

2. Match each response with its meaning.

   _____ a. NEW FILE   (1)   File is ready for editing.
                  :   *_   (2)   ED couldn't write a directory
   _____ b.   :   *_   entry for the temporary file.
                                         (3)   File was not found.
   _____ c. ** FILE IS READ/ONLY **   (4)   File has R/O status.
   _____ d. DISK OR DIRECTORY FULL   (5)   File has system status.

            A>_

3. Assume that you got the correct response and go on to the next step. Show the command to append all the lines. *_______________________________________

4. Match each response with its meaning.

   _____ a.   1: *_   (1)   No lines were appended.
                                      (2)   Some, but not all, lines were
   _____ b.   BREAK ">" AT A   appended.
                      :   *   (3)   All lines were appended.

5. Assume that all lines were appended and go on to the next step. Write one command to change ALL to SENIOR in line 1.

   *____

6. Write one command to insert NIGHTLY in line 3.

   *____

7. Write one command to insert the new fourth line. We still want the blank line before the start of the text of the memo.

   *____

   Remember that all your lines have now been renumbered.

8. Write one command to change BROUGHT to CALLED.

   *____

9. Write one command to position the character pointer after LIGHTS in the third point.

    *____

10. Write one command to delete EXCEPT THE CENTRAL HALL, leaving the

    period after LIGHTS. *____

11. Instead of questions 9 and 10, you could have used one J command to accomplish the same function. Show the command.

    *____

12. Write one command to insert the new step 4. Maintain the double-spacing before and after the line.

    *____

13. Write one command to change all the EXITs to DOOR.*_______________________

14. Write the commands to change 4 to 5, 5 to 6, and 6 to 7. (*Hint:* Step 5 is now on line 19.)

    *____

    *____

    *____

15. Write one command to delete the line containing VIOLATIONS WILL BE PUNISHED. (*Hint:* It's now line 26.)

    *____

16. Write one command to display the entire corrected file.

    *____

17. Write the command to end the edit normally and save your work.*______

18. Match these responses with their meanings.

    _______ a. A>_   (1) The file has been saved.

    _______ b. DISK OR DIRECTORY   (2) The source file was lost.
                FULL   (3) The editing work was lost.
                                       (4) The source file is still there.

19. Assuming you got a normal response, what files will appear on the disk directory?

    _______ a.   SECURITY.MEM

    _______ b.   SECURITY.DAT

    _______ c.   SECURITY.$$$

    _______ d.   SECURITY.BAK

20. Which of the above files contains the original text?

    ____

21. Which of the above files contains the new text?

    ____

22. Match the following commands with their functions.

    _______ a.   E   (1) Empty memory buffer.
                              (2) Finalize and rename $$$ file.
    _______ b.   H   (3) Rename source file as BAK file.
                              (4) Erase $$$ file.
    _______ c.   O   (5) New source file.
                              (6) Reopen old source file.
    _______ d.   Q   (7) Terminate ED.
                              (8) Continue ED.
    _______ e.   #

Self-Test Answer Key

1. A>ED SECURITY.MEM
2. a. 3
    b. 1
    c. 4
    d. 2
3. *#A
4. a. 3
    b. 2
5. *SALL^Z SENIOR
6. *JRE: ^Z NIGHTLY ^ZL
7. *4:IDATE: 5/14/82<CR>
8. *SBROUGHT^ZCALLED
9. *FLIGHTS
10. *D33 (Did you remember to delete the eight spaces preceding CENTRAL HALL, as well as the <CR><LF>?)

11. *JLIGHTS^Z^Z.

12. *17:I 4. TURN ON THE OUTSIDE LIGHTS.^L<CR>

13. *#SEXIT^ZDOOR

14. *19:S4^Z5
    *S5^Z6
    *S6^Z7

15. *26:K

16. *1:#T or *B#T

17. *E

18. a. 1, 4
    b. 3, 4

19. a, d (b could appear if it was present before editing)

20. d

21. a

22. a. 1, 2, 3, 7
    b. 1, 2, 3, 5, 8
    c. 1, 4, 6, 8
    d. 4, 7
    e. 1, 8

Suggested Machine Exercise

In this exercise you'll edit the PRACTICE.1 file that you created at the end of Chapter Eight. We'll leave you to decide what steps you want to follow. Be sure to practice using insert, delete, and the search and replace commands. The corrected copy is shown below.

```
THIS WAS A PRACTICE NEW FILE.
NOW IT'S A PRACTICE OLD FILE.
I AM EXPERIMENTING WITH ED'S
FILE EDITING FEATURES.
```

Save the edited file; you'll use it again at the end of Chapter Ten. You can erase PRACTICE.BAK.

CHAPTER TEN

Advanced ED Functions

You've now learned the basic ED commands and should be able to handle any editing function you need. However there are more facilities available under ED that make your job faster and easier. You'll learn those features in this chapter.

When you complete this chapter, you will be able to:

- Display the amount of space left in memory.
- Page through a file.
- Create and use combined commands.
- Create and use macros.
- Put ED to sleep.
- Create and use libraries.
- Place the revised file on a different disk.

TWO NEW COMMANDS

In this section, we'll introduce two new ED commands.

1.   When you're making major editing changes, you may want to check on your available memory buffer area. The command 0V (zero followed by V) will result in this display:

    free-space/total-space

For example, if your data space in your memory buffer is 30000 bytes and you've filled 20000 bytes with text lines, *0V would result in

    10000/30000

You've got 10,000 characters still available. You can now estimate how many more lines you can append or insert before running out of memory space.

(a) What command could result in the display shown below? *__________

    10000/12000

(b) How much free space is left? __________

(c) If you're working with lines that average 50 characters each, approximately how many more lines can you append or insert?

____

— — — — — — — — — —

(a) *0V (b) 10,000 bytes; (c) about 200

2. The P command causes ED to display a 23-line "page" and move the character pointer to the top of that page. The page size assumes that you have a 24-line video terminal and your text lines are less than or equal to your screen line length.

The format of the command is ±nP. The command 0P displays the next 23 lines and does not move the character pointer.

The simple command P displays 46 lines and moves the character pointer down 23 lines. On a 24-line screen the first 23 lines roll off the top, leaving the second 23 lines visible. The character pointer is pointing to the first *visible* line.

Suppose you want to scan your file at the video console. You want to scan pages of 23 lines each with the character pointer always pointing to the top screen line.

Your display looks like this:

```
A>ED INVENTY.DOC
   : *#A
  1: *_
```

(a) What command will display the first page? *__________

(b) Following the above command, what command will display the second page (lines 24 to 46)? *__________

(c) Following the above command, what command will display the third page (lines 47 to 69)? *__________

— — — — — — — — — —

(a) *0P or *23T (b) *P or *24:23T (c) *P or *47:23T

3.   The command –P displays the 46 lines preceding the character pointer and moves the character pointer back 23 lines. The effect is to move back one 23-line page.

(a)   Write a command to view the next page. *____________________________

(b)   Write a command to view the preceding page. *__________________________

— — — — — — — — — —

(a) *P (b) *–P

4.   The P command is meant for scanning pages on a 24-line video console, when each data line takes less than a full screen line.
  Under what conditions will P *not* have the intended effect?

_____ (a)   When the text lines are longer than video screen

_____ (b)   When the file contains more than 150 lines

_____ (c)   When the video console doesn't have 24 lines

_____ (d)   When the video console doesn't have upper case translation

— — — — — — — — — —

a, c

COMBINED COMMANDS

So far you have been using single ED commands. That is, you have typed and entered only one command at a time. But many ED commands can be combined so that you can accomplish several functions in one step. We'll show you how in the following frames.

5.   To combine commands, simply string them together on the command line following the *. ED will process the commands from left to right.
  For example, suppose you enter this command: –10L3K. ED will move the character pointer up 10 lines, then kill three lines. Note that the –10 goes with the L and the (+)3 goes with the K.

(a)   Write a command line to append 100 lines, move the character pointer

   down to the bottom, and display the last line. *____________________

(b)   Write a command to write 500 lines and display the amount of available

   space in memory. *____________________________________

————————————

(a) *100A-B-2T or *100A100:T (b) *500W0V

6. As you learned earlier, the F, S, N, I, and J commands all involve character strings. They can be combined with other commands, but you need to mark the end of each character string with Ctrl-Z. If the character string is not followed by another command, its end doesn't need to be marked. The final character string can be terminated by pressing Enter.

Here are some examples of combined commands containing character strings.

    *3FJONES^Z-3CIA<CR>

This command will find the third occurrence of JONES, back up the character pointer to a point in JONES, and insert an A. The final result will be JOANES.

    *3FJONES^Z-3CIA^Z3C-T<CR>

This will have the same effect. In addition, this command will move the character pointer to the end of the word, then display the entire line up to that point.

(a) Write a command to find the next occurrence of COST FACTOR and display the line up through the string.

    * ____

(b) Write a command to go to the beginning of memory, find the third occurrence of 1989, delete the 89, insert 90 instead, and display the corrected line.

    * ____

————————————

(a) *FCOST FACTOR^Z-T<CR> (b) *B3F1989^Z-2DI90^Z0LT<CR>

7. Your commands are getting longer now and it's time to mention the CP/M-86 limit on command length. A CP/M-86 command can contain up to 255 characters. ED places a further limit on F, S, N, and J commands; they are limited to 100 characters.

Suppose you want to search for this entire sentence:

NOW IS THE TIME FOR ALL GOOD MEN.

and replace it with this sentence:

THE QUICK BROWN FOX JUMPS.

Suppose also that your console has only 24 characters to a line. Use the boxes below to show how you would enter the command.

				1	:		*																

— — — — — — — — — —

				1	:		*	S	N	O	W		I	S		T	H	E		T	I	M	E

	F	O	R		A	L	L		G	O	O	D		M	E	N	.	^	Z	T	H	E	

Q	U	I	C	K		B	R	O	W	N		F	O	X		J	U	M	P	S	.		

8. Certain commands may not be combined with any others. They are: E, H, O and Q. When you want to terminate ED you must use a separate command to do it.

Which of the following commands can be used in combination?

____ (a) Q   ____ (e) K

____ (b) I   ____ (f) O

____ (c) P   ____ (g) H

____ (d) E   ____ (h) F

— — — — — — — — — —

(b), (c), (e), and (h)

9. Let's try some more combinations before going on.

(a) Write one command to append and display all the lines in a short file.

*____

(b) Write one command to append all the lines and display lines 100 through 120. *____

(c) Do you remember this problem? 2: 16 APPLE ST. Write one command to move the character pointer to line 2, then move it in nine characters, delete the next three characters, move it to the beginning of the line, and display the entire line. *____

(d) Do you remember this one? 5: MARY SMITH. Write one command to find MARY, insert ANN, and display the entire line. *____

(e) Write one command to insert a second line containing APT. #102 and display the first three lines.

*____

(f) Write a command to append all the lines, change all EXITs to DOOR, and display the entire file.

*____

— — — — — — — — —

(a) *#A#T (b) *#A100::120T (c) *2:9C3D2:T (d) *FMARY ^ZIANN ^Z0LT (e) *2:IAPT. #102^L^ZB3T (f) *#A#SEXIT^ZDOOR^ZB#T

MACROS

Sometimes you want to repeat a combined command more than once. You can write a macro and have it repeated any number of times. The following frames will show you how.

10. The format of an ED macro is nMcombined-command. ED will repeat the combined command, from left to right, the number of times you specify, or throughout the entire file if you use #.

For example, look at this macro: *5MF89^Z-2T. ED will find the next occurrence of "89" and display the two lines leading up to it. Then go on and find the next occurrence of "89" and display the two lines leading up to that. This will continue until the entire macro has been repeated, left to right, five times. This is quite different from the command *5F89^Z-2T which would find the fifth occurrence of 89 and display the two lines leading up to it. If a macro is combined with other commands, it must be the last part of the command line.

Match the commands below with their functions.

_____ (a) *B10LK

_____ (b) *B10MLK

_____ (c) *B10L10K

_____ (d) *B10M10L10K

1. Kill lines 2, 4, 6, 8, . . ., 20.
2. Kill lines 11 to 20, 31 to 40, 51 to 60, . . ., 191 to 200.
3. Kill lines 11 to 20.
4. Kill line 11.

— — — — — — — — — —

(a) 4; (b) 1; (c) 3; (d) 2

11. In a macro every character string must be terminated by Ctrl-Z, including the final one. Write a macro that will start at the beginning of the file, find every occurrence of 1989, and change the 89 to 90. Use the extended search capability of the N command.

* ____

— — — — — — — — — —

*B#MN1989^Z-2DI90^Z

Explanation:

B sends the character pointer to the beginning of the memory buffer.

#M causes the macro to be repeated up to 65535 times.

N1989 searches (extended) for the next occurrence of 1989. The character pointer is positioned after the matching string.

^Zmarks the end of the search string.

−2D deletes the preceding two characters which will always be "89."

I90 inserts 90 in front of the character pointer.

^Z terminates the 90.

12. If you omit the number in front of M the macro is repeated until some outside circumstance stops it. Usually it repeats until it encounters a command that it can no longer execute because it has reached the end of data in memory, the end of memory, or the end of the file.

(a) When will this macro end—*M66L3T?______________________

____

____

(b) When will this macro end—*MN1989^Z-4D?__________________

____

____

— — — — — — — — — —

(a) at the end of data in the memory buffer, when ED can't move down 66 more lines; (b) when the entire source file has been exhausted and ED can't find another 1989

13. A macro always ends on a BREAK message. Even if you limit the number of times it's executed, you'll still get a BREAK message.
   Suppose you have this display:

```
    1:  *3M66LT
   67:   TANDEM REPORT — PAGE 2
  133:   TANDEM REPORT — PAGE 3 (REVISED)
  199:   TANDEM REPORT — PAGE 3
BREAK "#" AT L
  199:  *_
```

What happened?

_____ (a)   The macro executed successfully.

_____ (b)   ED encountered some error and could not finish executing the macro.

— — — — — — — — — —

(a) (you can see that ED typed lines 67, 133, and 199 and left the character pointer at the beginning of line 199)

14.   Did you know that you can tell ED to go to sleep? The command is nZ. The n specifies the number of seconds ED should sleep. We use the Z command to force ED to pause for a specific period of time while processing a repetitive macro. This gives us time to cancel the macro if we want to.

For example, suppose we want to search the file for all occurrences of JONES and replace them with SMITH. However we want to take a cautious approach and view each JONES before it gets replaced. The command we might use is: *BMNJONES^Z-2T10Z-5DISMITH^Z-2T5Z<CR>. This will cause the following actions:

1.   Move the character pointer to the beginning of memory.
2.   Execute the macro until a BREAK occurs.
   a.   Search for the next occurrence of JONES.
   b.   Display the two lines preceding the found string, up through JONES.
   c.   Sleep 10 seconds, giving us a chance to read the displayed lines and cancel the command if we don't want the change to be made.
   d.   Delete JONES.
   e.   Insert SMITH.
   f.   Display the result.
   g.   Sleep another 5 seconds.
   h.   Repeat the macro.

We can abort a macro at any time by typing any character.

Suppose we want to search the entire file (not just memory) for the phrase COST PLUS. We're looking for a particular sentence that we want to change. We want to view each occurrence of COST PLUS for about 5 seconds. When we find the right sentence, we'll abort the command. Write the command to do this.

*____

— — — — — — — — — — —

*BMNCOST PLUS^Z-2T5Z<CR> (We recommend displaying two preceding lines in case the found string is at the beginning of a line. You'll get a better idea of the context with two lines.)

LIBRARIES

ED allows you to insert an existing file into your current file. We'll show you how to do this in the following frames.

15. To insert a file into the file you are editing use the ED command R (read). Its format is Rfile-identifier. If you omit the filetype, it's assumed to be LIB. The library file will be inserted in front of the character pointer.
   Suppose the disk contains a file named CONFID.LIB with this text:

```
1:    THIS REPORT IS COMPANY CONFIDENTIAL.
2:    DO NOT REMOVE FROM THE PREMISES.
```

(a) Now you're editing a file called ANNUAL.REP. Write the command to insert CONFID.LIB as lines 65 and 66.

   *____

(b) Write a command to insert FORMAT3.FMT at the character pointer.

   *____

— — — — — — — — — —

(a) *65:RCONFID (b) *RFORMAT3.FMT

16. If you want to use R in a combined command you must put Ctrl-Z after the file identifier or ED can't find the next command.
   ED will not accept a command in the format nRfilename. If you want to do multiple inserts, you can use R in a macro. The filename must be terminated with Ctrl-Z, even if it's the last command in the macro.

(a) Write the command to move down 64 lines, insert file JUNE.DAT, and display the preceding three lines.

   *____

(b) Write a macro to start at the beginning of memory and insert CONFID.LIB as every 65th and 66th line. Limit the macro to 10 iterations. (We'll explain why in frame 18.)

   *____

— — — — — — — — — —

(a) *64LRJUNE.DAT^Z-3T
(b) *B10M64LRCONFID^Z

17. You can also create a second file while editing. The command is nX file-identifier, where n indicates the number of lines to place in the file—starting at the character pointer, of course. The lines are not removed from the current file. For example, 20XTEMPFILE.LIB would write the next 20 lines to a new file called TEMPFILE.LIB. (LIB is not assumed in this command.)

If you use nX without a file identifier, a temporary file named X$$$$$$$.LIB is created.

The temporary file, named X$$$$$$$.LIB, can then be inserted in your current file by the simple command R. The filename is omitted when you want to reference X$$$$$$$.LIB. When followed by other commands, R should be terminated by Ctrl-Z so ED doesn't try to read the next characters as part of a filename.

You can use the temporary library facility to move or copy lines from one part of the file to another part of the same file.

Suppose you want to move paragraph 3, lines 15 to 20, to follow line 35. Write the commands to:

(a) Make lines 15 to 20 into a temporary LIB file. *_______________________

(b) Insert the temporary LIB file after line 35. *_______________________

(c) Delete lines 15 to 20. *_______________________

— — — — — — — — — —

(a) *15:6X or *15::20X (b) *36:R (c) *15:6K or 15::20K

18. The R command should be used cautiously in an unlimited macro. If ED reaches the end of data, it will continue to process the R command repeatedly until something stops it. It will fill your memory buffer with repetitions of the library file until memory is full or until you interrupt the process.

Suppose you want to repeat line 1 at the top of every page. (That is, after every 66th line.)

(a) Which of the following macros would be better?

    _____ A. *BXLM65LR^Z

    _____ B. *BXLM65LR^Z3T5^Z

(b) Explain your choice.

____

____

____

____

——————————

(a) B; (b) because it gives us a chance to identify when the end of the data has been reached and interrupt the macro

19.   If you issue a second X command for the same file identifier, the lines are *appended* to that file. The command 0X file-identifier will erase the indicated file. (You can erase any file this way.)
(a)   Write a command to clear the temporary LIB file and put lines 13 to 18 there.

*______________________________________

(b)   Write a command to erase the file named TEMPFILE.LIB.

*______________________________________

——————————

(a) *0X13::18X is one way to write the command; (b) *0XTEMPFILE.LIB

20.   The temporary LIB file is automatically erased only if you use either of the termination commands: E or Q. If you terminate by Ctrl-C the file will not be erased. You can erase it yourself or let the next edit session erase it. However if you use the X command again before the X$$$$$$$.LIB file is erased, remember that the lines will be added to the old file.

(a)   Suppose you terminate an edit session by Ctrl-C. You used the X command (without a file identifier) during the session. What files would you expect to see on the disk directory?

_____   A.   filename.typ

_____   B.   filename.BAK

_____   C.   filename.$$$

_____   D.   filename.LIB

_____   E.   X$$$$$$$.LIB

(b)   Write the command to erase the temporary LIB file.

A>______________________________________

(c)   Do H and O erase the temporary file?________________________________

——————————

(a) A, C, and E (you could have the other files if they were present before the edit);
(b) A>ERA X$$$$$$$.LIB (c) no

SPECIFYING THE NEW-FILE-IDENTIFIER

21.   If you want the edited file to appear on a different disk from the source file, use this command format:

>   d>ED filename d:

ED will open the $$$ file on the drive you specify as d:. As you know, this eventually becomes the edited file. The BAK file remains on the original disk.
  If you want to give the edited file a different name, use this command format:

>   d>ED old-file-identifier new-file-identifier

The old file will retain its original name and the edited version will take the new name. There won't be a BAK file created.

(a)   Write a command to edit INVENTY.DOC on A disk and place the edited file

on B disk. A>____

(b)   Write a command to edit MAILIST.DOC from B disk and place the file on A disk, calling it MAILABEL.

A>____

(c)   After the above edit, what will B:MAILIST.DOC be called?

____

(d)   Suppose you enter this command A>ED PRACTICE.1 B: and get this response: Output file exists, erase it. What do you suppose the message means?

____

____

— — — — — — — — — — —

(a) A>ED INVENTY.DOC B:
(b) A>ED B:MAILIST.DOC MAILABEL
(c) still B:MAILIST.DOC;
(d) there's already a PRACTICE.1 on disk B

22. Summary. In this chapter you've seen how to display memory space, move and display pages, write combined commands, write macros, create and use libraries, and create edited files on other disks. The commands you've studied are:

ED file-identifier d:	Put edited file on d:
ED old-file-id new-file-id	Call edited file by new-file-id
0V	Display available memory space
±nP	Move character pointer; display page
nM	Macro
Rfile-identifer	Insert file
R	Insert temporary file
nXfile-identifier	Put n lines in file
0Xfile-identifier	Erase a file

Chapter Ten Self-Test

1. Write a command to display the amount of memory space available.

   *____

2. Write a command to display the next 46 lines and move the character pointer down 23 lines.

   *____

3. Write a command to append the first 100 lines, replace all "*" with "JANET" and display all the lines.

   *____

4. Revise your above command so that 24 lines are displayed at a time, with a 30-second pause after each display.

   *____

5. Write a command to copy lines 1–5 100 times, starting on line 6.

   *____

6. Assume that you have just initiated ED and your memory buffer is empty. Write a command to completely search the source file substituting JOHN for the * character.

   *____

7. Write a command to copy the STARS.LIB file into your current file, beginning at line 100.

   *____

8. Write a command to copy the STARS.LIB file after every existing tenth line. (Don't count the lines that are added by the command.) Terminate the command after 10 iterations.

   *____

9. Revise the above command so that you can terminate it manually from the keyboard when it's obvious that the existing lines have been finished.

   *____

10. Write a command to append the next three lines to the file named

    BUILD.DAT. *____

11. Write a command to erase BUILD.DAT.

    *____

12. Write a command to erase any data in the temporary LIB file and write the next 100 lines into it.

    *____

Self-Test Answer Key

1. *0V
2. *P
3. *100A#S*^ZJANET^ZB#T
4. *100A#S*^ZJANET^ZBM24T30Z24L
5. *1::5X6:100MR^Z
6. *MN*^Z-DIJOHN^Z
7. *100:RSTARS
8. *10M10LRSTARS^Z
9. *M10LRSTARS ^Z-2T2T10Z
   (You may have chosen to display a different set of lines and to "sleep" a different number of seconds.)
10. *3XBUILD.DAT
11. *0XBUILD.DAT
12. *0X^Z100X

Suggested Machine Exercise

1. First of all, use ED to create a STARS.LIB file that contains two rows of asterisks.

2. Then edit the PRACTICE.1 file. Call the edited filed PRACTICE.2. It should currently contain four lines. Using a temporary LIB file, copy those four lines 100 times.

3. Your file should now contain 400 lines. Try using the P command to view them.

4. Use 0V to check your available memory space.

5. Now insert the STARS.LIB file after every fourth line so your whole file looks like this:

```
THIS WAS A PRACTICE NEW FILE.
NOW IT'S A PRACTICE OLD FILE.
I AM EXPERIMENTING WITH ED'S
FILE EDITING FEATURES.
*****************************
*****************************
```
(repeated 100 times)

6. Now see if you can enter a macro that will delete one row of stars from every set.

This concludes the machine exercise for this chapter. Save the PRACTICE.1 and PRACTICE.2 files to work with in Chapter Eleven. It doesn't matter what state PRACTICE.1 is in. You can erase the STARS.LIB file or experiment with it some more if you wish. When you're ready, go on to Chapter Eleven.

CHAPTER ELEVEN
Submitting Command Files

CP/M-86 commands are usually submitted one at a time. If you want to copy several specific files from one disk to another, you generally use several successive PIP commands. The CP/M-86 SUBMIT program allows you to submit a batch of commands at one time. Then all the commands are processed before control returns to you at the console.

In this chapter you'll learn to use the CP/M-86 SUBMIT command.

When you complete this chapter, you will be able to:

- Create a command file using symbolic parameters.
- Execute the command file using SUBMIT with actual parameters.

THE SUBMIT COMMAND

1. The SUBMIT command is used to execute all the commands in a file of filetype SUB. A SUB file always contains a list of CP/M-86 commands. You create the SUB file using ED. Let's assume, for now, that the SUBMIT.CMD file and the SUB file are both on disk A.

Here is an example, stored as the file CLEAN.SUB.

```
ERA *.BAK
DIR
```

The first command erases all files with filetype BAK. The second command simply displays a directory. The two commands will be executed by CP/M-86 when you enter the command SUBMIT CLEAN. Of course, SUBMIT.CMD must be on the default drive. Suppose file CLEAN2.SUB contains these commands:

```
ERA *.BAK
ERA *.REL
DIR
```

(a) What one command will execute all these?_________________________

(b) How is the effect different from the above example?_________________

(c)   Modify CLEAN2.SUB so that the size of each CMD file will be displayed instead of a complete directory.

____

____

— — — — — — — — — — —

(a) SUBMIT CLEAN2 (b) all existing REL files are erased as well; (c) eliminate DIR, use STAT *.CMD in its place

2.   A command file is a file with filetype SUB that is intended to be used with the SUBMIT command. The files CLEAN.SUB and CLEAN2.SUB are both command files. These are sometimes called submit files. The examples you just saw use CP/M-86 built in commands in the command file. Any CP/M-86 transient commands, such as PIP or STAT, or any other command (CMD file) can also be included in a command file. We'll soon see how to specify parameters and line entries when a file is submitted.

   Suppose you copy the same four files (PIP, STAT, NEWDISK, and COPYDISK) onto every new disk you use.

(a)   Write a command file that you could execute with SUBMIT SETUPDSK to copy the four files onto drive B from the current drive.

____

____

____

____

(b)   What is the name of the file you have created?

____

— — — — — — — — — — —

(a)   PIP B:=PIP.CMD
      PIP B:=STAT.CMD
      PIP B:=NEWDISK.CMD
      PIP B:=COPYDISK.CMD
(b)   SETUPDSK.SUB

SYMBOLIC PARAMETERS

3. Often the information you need in a command file may vary from one submission to the next. For example, if your system includes more than two drives, you may want to be able to specify the destination drive, as in SETUPDSK.SUB in the preceding frame, when you SUBMIT the command file. You can do this with symbolic parameters. The first symbolic parameter in a command file is indicated by $1; the second by $2, etc. You would need only one to turn SETUPDSK into a more flexible file.

```
PIP $1:=PIP.CMD
PIP $1:=STAT.CMD
PIP $1:=ED.CMD
PIP $1:=COPYDISK.CMD
```

Notice that the symbolic parameter $1 is used in place of a drivename. The actual parameter, a valid drivename, is supplied with the SUBMIT command like this:

```
SUBMIT SETUPDSK B
```

This command will insert "B" wherever the first symbolic parameter appears in SETUPDSK.SUB and execute the commands as if each specified drive B instead of $1. Notice that we followed each symbolic parameter in the command file with the colon (:) that is needed for a drivename in the SUB file. If the colon were omitted there it would need to be included following the drivename in the SUBMIT command.

(a) What command could execute the command file SETUPDSK, as shown above, copying the files onto drive C?

____

(b) Which element in SETUPDSK.SUB above is a symbolic parameter?______

(c) If a submit file required two symbolic parameters, what would the name of

the second one be?____

— — — — — — — — — — —

(a) SUBMIT SETUPDSK C (b) $1; (c) $2

4. Submit files can contain any combination of commands. Here is a list of commands that could be used to assemble a file of type A86, erase any backup files, copy the file produced by ASM86 to another drive and erase the original file.

```
ASM86 $1
ERA *.BAK
PIP $2:=$1.LST
ERA $1.LST
```

This file could be named ASSEMBLE.SUB. Two parameters are needed in the SUBMIT command to execute it. The first parameter is the filename of the program to be assembled. You specify only the first part, as it is always type A86. The second parameter names the drive on which you want to save the LST file. Suppose the assembly language program is in file INVENT.A86. You want the LST file saved on drive B.

(a) Write a command to execute ASSEMBLE.SUB

A>____

(b) Modify the file or the invoking command so the LST file is printed rather than saved on drive B.

____

— — — — — — — — — — — —

(a) SUBMIT ASSEMBLE INVENT B
(b) change the PIP command to PIP LST:=$1.LST—to do this without changing the file, you could use SUBMIT ASSEMBLE INVENT LST

5. When designing symbolic parameters, make the ones you might want to omit the higher ones. For example, here are two versions of a file called PROTECT.SUB.

Good	*Poor*
STAT $2$1 $$R/O	STAT $1$2 $$R/O
DIRS $2	DIRS $1

It's better to make the drivename the larger parameter so that it can be omitted when the default drive is desired. In the "poor" version, if you want to protect SEARCH.CMD on the default drive, you must enter

A>PROTECT A: SEARCH.CMD

You cannot omit the drivename or STAT would interpret SEARCH.CMD as $1. In the "good" version, you can enter

    A>PROTECT SEARCH.CMD

The drivename can be omitted because it is the final parameter.

(a) Code a submit file to PIP a file from one location to another. The following parameters should be symbolic: source drive, destination drive, source file identifier, and destination file identifier.

____

(b) Code a submit file to display both directories and the file status for a generalized file identifier. The file identifier and its drivename should both be symbolic.

____

____

____

— — — — — — — — — — — —

(a) we would do it this way: PIP $1$4=$3$2 and call it COPY.SUB (This way, we can enter A>SUBMIT COPY B: SEARCH.DAT and the command that will be executed is PIP B:=SEARCH.DAT. We can add a source drivename, as in A>SUBMIT COPY B: SEARCH.DAT C: and the command will be PIP B:=C:SEARCH.DAT. Finally, we can use all four parameters, as in A>SUBMIT COPY B: SEARCH.DAT C: LOOK.DAT and the command will be PIP B:LOOK.DAT=C:SEARCH.DAT.)

(b) We would do it this way: DIR $2$1
                                 DIRS $2$1
                                 STAT $2$1

SUBMIT PROCESSING

6. Let's look at what actually happens when you enter a SUBMIT command. First of all, the system associates any actual parameters in your SUBMIT command line with the numbered symbolic parameters in the command file. If you don't use the same number of parameters in your command as there are symbolic parameters in the file, the extra parameters are ignored. This could result in an INVALID FORMAT message for some of the commands.

The submit function proceeds to create a file named $$$.SUB. This file contains all the commands with the actual parameters filled in. Suppose the command SUBMIT SETUPDSK B were entered as in frame 3. The $$$.SUB file is created, using parameter B to replace $1 wherever it appears. The $$$.SUB file looks like this:

```
PIP B:=PIP.CMD
PIP B:=STAT.CMD
PIP B:=ED.CMD
PIP B:=SYSTEM.CMD
```

SUBMIT always places this file on drive A, no matter which drive is default and no matter which drive contains SUBMIT.CMD or the SUB file. So, if disk A is write protected or R/O, you can't use SUBMIT.

The SUBMIT program then executes the $$$.SUB file. The last step of processing a $$$.SUB file is to erase it. Consider the file ASSEMBLE.SUB from the previous frame.

(a) What happens if you enter SUBMIT ASSEMBLE PROGRAM?

____

(b) What is the name of the intermediate submit file created by CP/M-86?

____

(c) Write the contents of the intermediate file if you use SUBMIT ASSEMBLE PROGRAM B.

____

____

____

____

(d) When is the intermediate file processed?

____

(e) Where is the intermediate file stored?

____

(f) When is the intermediate file erased?

____

— — — — — — — — — —

(a) some error will occur because you gave only one parameter. The error will be an INVALID FORMAT on PIP.; (b) $$$.SUB

(c)   ASM PROGRAM
      ERA *.BAK
      PIP B:=PROGRAM.LST
      ERA PROGRAM.LST

(d) immediately; (e) drive A; (f) after it is processed

7. When you use SUBMIT, you may occassionally get effects you don't expect. Suppose, for example, you have a command file that copies all the files from disk A to disk B. The $$$.SUB file includes the command PIP B:=A:*.*. All the files will be copied to the B disk—including the $$$.SUB file! When SUBMIT terminates, it will erase $$$.SUB from drive A but not drive B. You'll need to erase that one yourself.

Suppose a command file COPY.SUB includes these commands:

```
PIP $1=A:*.*
DIR $1:
STAT $1:
```

(a) What command would you use for a copy to disk C?

____

(b) After the SUBMIT program terminates normally, where will you have the $$$.SUB file?

____

(c) What sort of command, added to the file above, would eliminate the $$$.SUB file from the destination disk before the SUBMIT terminates?

____

— — — — — — — — — —

(a) SUBMIT COPY C (b) on the C disk; (c) a command to erase $$$.SUB on $1 drive

8. We've seen what happens when you use the SUBMIT command. Now let's take a closer look at the SUB file—what you can put into it and what it can do. We said that any CP/M-86 commands, built-in or transient, can be used. Any command that invokes a CMD file is valid. Any of the parameters can be replaced by symbolic parameters in the SUBMIT file. Normally a command line you enter at the console is processed by the CCP. Any parameters you can include in such a command line can be replaced with symbolic parameters and provided when the file is submitted.

You may want to store a dollar sign in a file to be submitted. Since the dollar sign character ($) generally indicates a symbolic parameter, you need to tell SUBMIT if it means something else. You do this by using a double dollar sign ($$) which SUBMIT reduces to a single symbol. For example, to erase a file named THANK.$$$ from within a SUBMIT command file, you write one of these commands:

```
ERA THANK.$$*
ERA THANK.$$$$$$
```

You do not use ERA THANK.$$$, as SUBMIT cannot relate that to the file.
   Suppose MIXTURE.SUB contains these four lines:

```
ERA $1:*.DAT
$3
PIP $1:=*.DAT[$2]
REN KEEP.SUB=$$$.SUB
```

The command SUBMIT MIXTURE B U is issued.

(a) Rewrite the last line so it is valid.

___

(b) Suppose the command file contains only the last two lines—corrected. Write a command to execute it using the B disk as the destination. Specify that all characters will be converted to lowercase on the B disk.

___

(c) How will you be able to find the data in $$$.SUB after the CCP regains control?

___

— — — — — — — — — —

(a) REN KEEP.SUB=$$$$$$.SUB (b) SUBMIT MIXTURE B L (c) KEEP.SUB is still available

LINE INPUT

9. We've been dealing with commands that run to completion without any console interaction. Often we need to use commands that require some type of input from the console. (NEWDISK and COPYDISK are good examples.) Line input for the CP/M-86 transient commands and other transient programs must be supplied by the user when the program is executed. The console interaction will be just the same as if you entered the commands individually. All the commands and messages are displayed as the submit file is processed so that you can tell where the system is in the process and when you must respond. The console screen looks just as it does when the commands are entered one at a time.

Built-in commands are different. When the separate command ERA *.* is issued, the question ALL FILES? (Y/N) is displayed. SUBMIT reads the *next line* in the submit file to answer this question automatically. So if you put ERA *.* in your submit file, make the next line Y (for yes).

(a)   Which of the CP/M-86 commands below is likely to require some line input?

    _____ A.   ED NEW.FIL

    _____ B.   ERA *.CMD

    _____ C.   NEWDISK B: $DS

    _____ D.   COPYDISK

    _____ E.   STAT *.*

(b)   Suppose you are executing a command file and see this displayed:

```
A>PIP B:=STAT.CMD
```

What must you do?____

(c)   Suppose you see this displayed while a command file is executing:

```
A>ERA *.*
ALL   (Y/N)?_
```

What must you do to erase all the files?_____________________________

— — — — — — — — — —

(a) A, C, and D; (b) nothing, just wait; (c) nothing, just wait

10.   Let's look at a complete screen display and interaction under SUBMIT. Suppose COPY.SUB contains these commands:

```
ERA   $1:*.*
Y
PIP   $1:=A:*.*
ERA   $1:$$*.SUB
DIR   $1:
```

You enter SUBMIT COPY B to execute the file. You then see this on the screen (the A> prompt comes up first, then the rest).

```
A>ERA B:*.*
ALL (Y/N)?_
```

SUBMIT then reads the next line and answers its own question. Then it picks up the next command. You see this:

```
A>PIP B:=A:*.*
COPYING_
```

The list of files copied is displayed on your screen.

(a)   What is displayed next? A>_______________________________________

(b)   Then what? A>____

(c)   What is the final display resulting from the COPY command file?

____

_ _ _ _ _ _ _ _ _ _ _

(a) A>ERA B:$*.SUB (the $$ has been reduced); (b) A>DIR B: (c) the directory from disk B

Any CP/M-86 commands (CMD file references) can be included in SUBMIT files. You can even include a SUBMIT command as the last command in a SUB file. This allows you to chain separate groups of commands. However you should not try such a technique until you are at ease with the unchained SUBMIT.

You have seen how to use SUBMIT for batch processing of CP/M-86 commands. You'll get a chance to build and execute a command file in the suggested machine exercise for this chapter.

Chapter Eleven Self-Test

1.   Write a command file named FIXUP.SUB that will accomplish the following on the originating disk.

   - Rename the BAK file of a filename (use a symbolic parameter) to have filetype OLD.
   - Erase all BAK files.
   - Display the disk status.

____

____

____

2. Write a command to process the file you created in question 1 saving PERSNL.BAK file as PERSNL.OLD.

3. What would you expect to happen if you omit the symbolic parameter in the SUBMIT command?

4. Assuming you entered a valid SUBMIT command, write out the contents of the temporary file.

5. What is the name of this temporary file?

6. Suppose you create FIXUP.SUB on drive B and submit it from there. Where will the temporary file be stored?

7. Write a command file to accomplish the following:

    - Erase all files on the specified drive. (Use a symbolic parameter for drivename.)
    - Copy disk A to the specified drive, using COPYDISK.
    - Remove the temporary SUB file from the specified drive.
    - Display a directory and status of the specified drive.

8. Suppose your file from question 7 is named BACKUP.SUB and you wish to use it to duplicate your disk onto drive C. Write the command.

9. Consider the file you wrote in question 7 above. Which commands require that you make some line input from the console?

Self-Test Answer Key

1. REN $1.OLD=$1.BAK
   ERA *.BAK
   STAT

2. SUBMIT FIXUP PERSNL

3. An error in processing the REN command. (INVALID FORMAT)

4. REN PERSNL.OLD=PERSNL.BAK
   ERA *.BAK
   STAT

5. $$$.SUB

6. Drive A

7. ERA $1:*.*
   Y
   COPYDISK
   ERA $1:$$*.SUB
   DIR $1:
   STAT $1:

8. SUBMIT BACKUP C

9. COPYDISK

Suggested Machine Exercise

Before you begin this exercise make sure that you have a disk containing SUBMIT.CMD. The same disk should contain PRACTICE.1 which you edited in the last chapter. You'll need a scratch disk with nothing important on it, as well.

1.   For the first exercise use ED to build FIXUP.SUB containing the commands you wrote for Self-Test question 1. SUBMIT that file to save PRACTICE.BAK as PRACTICE.OLD and get rid of other BAK files.

   Be sure this is working successfully before you continue with the next exercise.

2.   For the second exercise use ED to build BACKUP.SUB, which you wrote in Self-Test question 7. Most important: Be sure to put the symbolic parameter in the ERA command or you'll do terrible things to the data on your A disk! Submit that file for drive B. Be sure you have a dispensable disk in drive B before you SUBMIT the file. If you get errors, re-edit the file to clean up the commands.

Postword

This completes our self-teaching guide on CP/M-86. You've learned how to use all the built-in commands and most of the transient commands. We've omitted the commands that pertain specifically to 8086 assembly language programming. Appendix B contains a summary of all the commands you've studied in this book. We suggest you cut out Appendix B and keep it near your console.

Good Luck!

APPENDIX A
PIP Parameters

Format	Function
*B	Block mode copy; copies blocks of data signaled by ^S character
Dn	Delete characters after column n
E	Echo on console
F	Filter form feeds
*H	Transfer and check hex data; remove unnecessary characters and display errors on console
*I	Ignore :00 records in H type transfer (I implies H so don't use both)
L	Translate letters to lowercase
N	Insert line numbers
N2	Insert line numbers and expand all tabs to next eighth column
*O	Non-ASCII file copy; ignore end-of-file marks (^Z)
Pn	Insert form feed every n lines; if n is omitted, 60 is assumed
Q*string* ^Z	Quit copying after string
S*string* ^Z	Start copying with string
Tn	Expand tab characters to every nth column
U	Translate letters to uppercase
*V	Read new file to verify
*Z	Zero parity bit on input

*Not covered in this book.

APPENDIX B

Reference Summary

[( ) indicates optional operands.]

BUILT-IN COMMANDS

Format	*Function*
ERA *file-identifier*	Erase named file(s)
DIR *(file-identifier)*	Display nonsystem directory
DIRS *(file-identifier)*	Display system directory
REN *new-specific-identifier=old-specific-identifier*	Change name of file
TYPE *specific-identifier*	Display contents of file
USER *user-number*	Change user number

TRANSIENT COMMANDS

Format	*Function*
ASM86 *file-identifier*	Assemble A86 file
ASSIGN *logical-device physical-device*	Change logical device assignment
COPYDISK	Copy a disk
DDT86 *file-identifier*	Debug a program
ED *specific-file-id (d:) (new-file-id)*	Edit specified file
FUNCTION	Program the function keys
GENCMD *file-identifier*	Create a CMD file
HELP *(topic (subtopic))*	Display information about topic
NEWDISK *drivename: option*	Format a new disk
PIP	Enter PIP command level
PIP *destination=source([parameters])*	Copy a file from source to destination
PROTOCOL *protocol*	Specify protocol for serial port
SPEED *characteristics*	Define communication characteristics for serial port
STAT	Display status of disk(s)
STAT *d:*=R/O	Set drive to read-only
STAT *file-identifier* ($SIZE)	Display status of file(s)
STAT *file-identifier* ($R/O $R/W $SYS $DIR)	Change status of file(s)
STAT *d:*USER:	Display user numbers
STAT *d:*DSK:	Display disk characteristics
SUBMIT *filename (parameters)*	Execute file of CP/M-86 commands
TOD (P)	Display date and time
TOD *mm/dd/yy hh:mm:ss*	Set date and time

ED commands and CP/M-86 control characters follow. PIP parameters are shown in Appendix A.

ED COMMANDS

Format	*Function*
ED *specific-file-id (d:) (new-file-id)*	Initiate ED
nA	Append n lines
±B	Move character pointer to beginning or end
±nC	Move character pointer n characters
±D	Delete n characters
E	Save file and end Ed
F*string*	Find string (use "f" for lowercase)
H	Save file and restart ED
I<CR>	Enter insert level (use "i" for lowercase)
I*string*^Z	Insert string (use "i" for lowercase)
I*string*<CR>	Insert string and <CR><LF> (use "i" for lowercase)
J*search-string*^Z*insert-string*^Z*delete-string*	Juxtapose and delete
±nK	Kill n lines
±nL	Move character pointer n lines
nM	Execute macro n times
N*string*	Extended find string (use "n" for lowercase)
O	Return to original file
±nP	Display pages
Q	Quit
R	Read temporary library file
R*specific-filename*	Read specified file
S*delete-string*^Z*insert-string*	Substitute (use "s" for lowercase)
±nT	Type n lines
±U	Uppercase translation
±V	Line numbering
nW	Write n lines
nX(*specific-file-identifier*)	Append n lines to specified file
0X(*specific-file-identifier*)	Erase specified file
nZ	Sleep n seconds
±n	Move n lines and type
n:	Move to line n
:n	Through line n

CP/M-86 CONTROL CHARACTERS

Format	*Function*
Ctrl-C	Cancel and restart
Ctrl-E	Start new line
Backspace (or Ctrl-H)	Backspace
Ctrl-I	Tab
Ctrl-J	Same as Enter
Ctrl-L	Substitute <CR><LF>
Ctrl-M	Same as Enter
Ctrl-P	Echo print
Ctrl-R	Reshow line
Ctrl-S	Suspend output
Ctrl-U	Delete line
Ctrl-X	Delete line
Ctrl-Z	String terminator
Del	Delete and display previous character
PrtSc	Print screen
Ctrl-Alt-Del	Reboot
Enter	Transmit a line

Index